BECOMING

Paul Avis, one of Anglicanism's leading ecclesiologists, has provided a great gift to anyone called to become a bishop. With a remarkably light touch, he has applied his considerable scholarship to the lived realities of episcopal ministry, combining a deep understanding of the shape of the Church with pearls of practical wisdom drawn from years of observing bishops in a host of different contexts. The result is an attractive and accessible study that will help bishops from churches across the world to go on becoming more fully the bishops God has called them to be.

Christopher Cocksworth, Bishop of
Coventry, Church of England

In 2013, the Anglican Church of Southern Africa declared that year 'A Year of Theological Education'. This raised untapped financial resources for our province but also laid bare the dearth in levels of understanding what the Church is and in particular, the episcopate. Our synodical structures addressed these questions by setting up, among others, the Canon Law Council to educate bishops and others about church order. In fact, a far cry from the people's wrestling. All they were yearning for was an account of what is a bishop and the bishop's role in democratic Southern Africa as we together lead the church's mission? Paul's book is the resource we were searching for. *Becoming a Bishop* is clearly and effectively written, theologically rigorous and yet accessible book. It is imbued with pastoral wisdom and will be helpful to the bishops of the Anglican Communion around the world, and indeed to bishops and those likely to be bishops of all Christian tradition. At home, it will aptly address the questions our year of theological education raised and equip not only bishops but all the Laos. I highly recommend *Becoming a Bishop*. I will in the first instance purchase a copy for each bishop within my province so that they may benefit from this well of wisdom.

Thabo Makgoba, Archbishop of Cape Town,
Anglican Church of Southern Africa

Becoming a Bishop is a worthy book for the person just elected to episcopal office and for the bishop approaching their silver anniversary. It is so because it invites the reader to enter afresh the living tradition of episcopal ministry. In particular, I found Paul Avis's exposition of the public, personal and private life of the bishop to be invitational, so that the reader really wants to grow into the fullness of their vocation. The author reminds us that episcopal ministry involves teaching, sanctifying and governing, yet he never loses sight of the humanity of the bishop. Not only is this a helpful book for bishops, new and experienced; it is also a book I recommend to dioceses which are praying for the right appointment or election that they may be served well and the flock of Christ kept together. The chapter on the collaborative ministry of bishops could well be enjoyed by bishops on retreat or at a study conference.

Victoria Matthews, Bishop of Christ Church, Anglican Church in Aotearoa, New Zealand and Polynesia

Paul Avis has hit the nail squarely on the head! In *Becoming a Bishop*, he invites the reader to reflect on the order and ministry of bishop. He suggests – rightly, I believe – that the church should primarily think about episcopacy in terms of a reasoned consideration of scripture, tradition and ecumenical agreements, all in light of God's mission for the church and the world. This book will make an invaluable resource for bishops and all with a stake in the mission and ministry of the church. Highly recommended.

Franklin Brookhart, Bishop of Montana, The Episcopal Church, USA

BECOMING A BISHOP

Theological Handbook of
Episcopal Ministry

Paul Avis

Bloomsbury T&T Clark
An imprint of Bloomsbury Publishing Plc

B L O O M S B U R Y
LONDON · NEW DELHI · NEW YORK · SYDNEY

Bloomsbury T&T Clark

An imprint of Bloomsbury Publishing Plc

Imprint previously known as T&T Clark

50 Bedford Square	1385 Broadway
London	New York
WC1B 3DP	NY 10018
UK	USA

www.bloomsbury.com

BLOOMSBURY, T&T CLARK and the Diana logo are trademarks of Bloomsbury Publishing Plc

First published 2015

British Library Cataloguing-in-Publication Data
A catalogue record for this book is available from the British Library.

ISBN:	HB:	978-0-567-65728-2
	PB:	978-0-567-65727-5
	ePDF:	978-0-567-65730-5
	ePub:	978-0-567-65729-9

Library of Congress Cataloging-in-Publication Data
Avis, Paul D. L.
Becoming a bishop : theological handbook of
episcopal ministry / by Paul Avis. – 1st [edition].
pages cm
Includes index.
ISBN 978-0-567-65727-5 (pbk) – ISBN 978-0-567-65728-2 (hbk) –
ISBN 978-0-567-65729-9 (epub) – ISBN 978-0-567-65730-5 (epdf)
1. Episcopacy. 2. Bishops. I. Title.
BV670.3.A95 2015
262'.12–dc23
2014048281

Typeset by Integra Software Services Pvt. Ltd.
Printed and bound in India

CONTENTS

FOREWORD

'Episcopally led, synodically governed', 'bishop-in-synod', 'the historic episcopate locally adapted' all mark out the centrality of episcopacy within the Anglican tradition. It is central to our self-understanding as Anglicans, central to our ecclesiology and central to our system of church government. The Anglican Communion today is defined by the Archbishop of Canterbury as Focus of Unity, and three Instruments of Communion, two of which, Lambeth Conferences and Primates' meetings, are also episcopal, and the third, the Anglican Consultative Council, involves bishops alongside laity and clergy in its membership.

The Lambeth Quadrilateral speaks of the Episcopal office 'locally adapted', and that local adaptation has taken many different forms throughout the Communion: from single bishops exercising oversight in sparsely populated dioceses to primates without any diocesan responsibility; from missionary bishops extending the frontiers of Christian witness; to part-time bishops exercising their ministry while engaged in administrative work or teaching in a seminary. Yet the ministry is at heart the same – leadership in ministry and mission within the Church of God.

Mission and ministry go hand in hand in today's Church. These twin themes shape this book. The bishop exercises leadership in the local church, the diocese, and relates that diocese to the wider church through its councils and synods, always seeking 'unity in truth' as Dr Avis describes it. This will bring the bishop into pastoral care, ecumenical conversations, disciplinary matters, teaching and public witness. Understanding the theological foundations of this ministry is vital, and that is what this book provides.

How does the individual bishop understand his or her own ministry? Are there common strands to all episcopal ministries? How do we relate the theology of episcopacy to the day-to-day office and work of a bishop in the twenty-first century? This is the task Dr Avis has undertaken for us, and we are deeply in his debt. Drawing on his deep knowledge of ecclesiology and his experience of supporting and encouraging all forms of ministry in the Church, he maps out a modern and realistic theological framework for the ministry of a bishop and relates this to the day-to-day work of ministry in the Church of God.

Having commissioned this study as the Secretary General of the Anglican Communion, I now find myself re-reading it as a bishop-elect in the Church of Ireland. Looking at it again from that new perspective, I am more than ever persuaded that the bishops of the Anglican Communion, wherever in the world they may be, will find it a source of wisdom and insight for their ministry. And, more than that, I am sure that bishops in other episcopally ordered churches will find that it speaks to their situation too.

The Right Revd Dr Kenneth Kearon, Bishop of Limerick and Killaloe, Church of Ireland; former Secretary General of the Anglican Communion

PREFACE

When Archbishop of Canterbury Michael Ramsey came to write his brief chapter 'The Bishop' in his much valued little book *The Christian Priest Today*, he lamented the scarcity of books about the office and work of a bishop. Legions of books had been written about episcopacy, he said, but 'few or none about the inner life or the practical problems of being a bishop at the present time'.[1] This current *Handbook* is a modest attempt to meet one part, but only one part, of the need identified by Archbishop Ramsey. It does concern the office and work of a bishop in the Church of God, though it does not presume to venture very far into the 'inner life' of the bishop. The main focus is on the *ministerial identity* of the bishop, especially the tasks and roles that belong to episcopacy. This is not really a 'how to do it' guide – though it is quite practical in places – but a *Theological Handbook*; that is to say a theological account of episcopal ministry. It aims to set the vital work of a bishop within the kind of ecclesiological framework that alone can make good Christian sense of it. It locates the bishop within the Church, within the purposes of God.

1. Michael Ramsey, *The Christian Priest Today* (revised edition, London: SPCK, 1985), p. 94. The present study is not the only current attempt to remedy this lack. Bishop David Tustin's *A Bishop's Ministry: Reflections and Resources for Church Leadership* (2013) is intentionally designed for Church of England bishops. David Tustin has provided a thoroughly useful and practical companion for new bishops and those bishops already in post who may want to review their ministry and reassess their priorities. His book is full of fascinating practical examples drawn from his own ministry. The comprehensive discussion ranges from pastoral issues and prayer to liturgical vesture and the organization of time, including time with the family (for married bishops) and time off duty. The approach is consistently sane, sensible and down to earth, but without taking his eyes off the spiritual horizon and divine calling. David Tustin draws from a wide range of relevant documents in the ecumenical domain, Roman Catholic and Lutheran, as well as Anglican, and the text is enriched by substantial quotations from Pope Gregory the Great's treatise on pastoral care (*Liber Regulae Pastoralis*) and St Bernard of Clairvaux's advice to bishops, which run like a golden thread through the book. Anglican bishops – and indeed bishops and potential bishops of other Christian world families and traditions – will find much there to ponder.

This book has been written in the conviction that bishops, like all Christians, are lifelong learners, that 'becoming a bishop' is an ongoing task of spiritual, theological and moral formation and always remains unfinished business – just as we all remain, as Christians in this life, unfinished people. Abbot André Louf wrote, 'How can we attune ourselves to grace? It always takes a lifetime to do – and this because God wants it so.'[2] God knows that we need time to be formed by grace into what our vocation demands. A bishop's calling involves a life-long process of conversion. St Anthony, the founder of desert spirituality, said, 'Every morning again I say to myself, Today I start.'[3]

My hope for this book is that it will lead bishops, and others who use it, back to the Scriptures and to the rich tradition of the Church and specifically to the doctrinal, liturgical and spiritual heritage of Anglicanism. I hope that my book will prove to be a useful companion, a *vade mecum*, in a bishop's work, helping bishops around the world to be more effective in the service of God and the Church – more focused on the essentials of episcopal ministry and more intentional in their practice. Although there is inevitably an Anglican emphasis in what follows, I believe that the theological resources that are provided here in support of episcopal ministry are of wider, indeed ecumenical relevance. There is no such animal as a purely 'Anglican' or 'Episcopal' bishop – a bishop is a bishop in the Church of God, and episcopal ministry is essentially and theologically the same, whatever Christian tradition it may be exercised within.

I am very conscious of the limitations of my own perspective. Firstly, I write as a priest, presbyter, not as a bishop. Although I have had many opportunities to observe bishops singly and collectively at close quarters – and always found that experience instructive, one way or another – I do not know what it feels like from the inside to be a bishop. Secondly, I write from a particular Anglican perspective, that of the Church of England. In spite of frequent travels in the Anglican Communion, I have limited knowledge of the distinctive ways and practices of some member Churches of the Communion. I am well aware that the lived experience of being a bishop varies from one part of the Communion to another. On the other hand, I am convinced that both the theology of episcopacy and the skills and aptitudes needed to be an effective bishop are, in essence, the same everywhere. What differs

2. André Louf, *Tuning into Grace: The Quest for God* (Kalamazoo, MI: Cistercian Publications, 1992), p. viii.

3. Louf, *Tuning into Grace: The Quest for God*, p. 6.

is the context – and every context is unique. So any book about the bishop's ministry that tried to be entirely practical could only be of local relevance. It would inevitably be parochial. Bishops in other contexts would find it annoyingly detached from their immediate reality. This book does not attempt to second-guess what sort of approach would be appropriate in any particular context. Rather, it aspires to set out some theological principles that might underpin episcopal ministry. However, it tries to do that in a way that is not divorced or removed from episcopal practice, in an ivory tower way, but informs and shapes practice.

The cameos – snapshots – that I have requested from Anglican bishops in various parts of the Communion have contributed to the shaping of this book, giving me a sense of what it is to be a bishop in diverse contexts and I hope helping to compensate for the limitations of my own perspective. I am hugely grateful to those bishops who agreed to contribute in this way: Archbishop Bernard Ntahoturi (Burundi) and Bishops Howard Gregory (Jamaica), Helen-Ann Hartley (Waikato, Anglican Church in Aotearoa, New Zealand and Polynesia), Stephen Andrews (Algoma, Anglican Church of Canada), William Franklin (Western New York, The Episcopal Church) and Surya Prakash (Church of South India). The six cameos are published on the companion website, and will be joined by reviews of this book and updates of study material. The website will enable this book to be treated for the time being as a rolling document, which can be corrected, supplemented and improved as bishops and others around the Communion read it and send me comments and insights from their particular contexts. For the cameos and related additional material please go to http://www.bloomsbury.com/uk/becoming-a-bishop-9780567657275/ and select the online resources tab.

The idea for this book came from the then Secretary-General of the Anglican Communion, the Revd Canon Dr Kenneth Kearon, in collaboration with the then Director for Unity, Faith and Order for the Communion, the Revd Canon Dr Alyson Barnett-Cowan. It was made possible by my secondment as General Secretary of the Council for Christian Unity, Church House, Westminster, UK, for a period spanning 2011 and 2012, to serve as Theological Consultant to the Anglican Communion Office, London. I acknowledge with warm thanks the helpful comments and advice on successive drafts, received from Canon Kearon, Canon Barnett-Cowan, Bishop Franklin Brookhart, Bishop Linda Nicholls, Bishop James Tengatenga, Dr Karen West, Canon Christopher Irvine, Canon Professor Katherine Grieb, Bishop Clayton Matthews and Bishop John Bauerschmidt and their colleagues on the board of the College for Bishops of the Episcopal Church. I was able to use some of the material at the Canterbury Cathedral school for new bishops early in 2014, and it was a privilege to give addresses, based on this book, at the retreat of the bishops of the Province of the Church in the West Indies at the Our Lady of Florida (Passionist) Spiritual Center, North Palm Beach, Florida, USA, in September 2014 and to receive useful feedback.[4] The views expressed in this book remain entirely my own. Biblical quotations are from the New Revised Standard Version, unless otherwise noted.

Paul Avis
reception@leahill.co.uk
September 2014

---

4. I regret that in writing this book I was unable to benefit from Christopher Beeley's, *Leading God's People: Wisdom from the Early Church for Today* (Grand Rapids, MI: Eerdmans, 2012), which came to my attention when my book was in press.

Chapter 1

THE OFFICE AND WORK OF A BISHOP IN THE CHURCH OF GOD

Becoming a Bishop

'How can I become a bishop?', someone might be wondering. Well, one way is via the internet. Send off your money and get a certificate by return stating that you are now a bishop (though of no known church). Now all you need is a flock, a diocese! Another route is to apply to be considered in one of the mainstream churches (but first make sure that it is a church that actually has bishops – some do not). Even in the rather traditional Church of England, you can actually apply to be a bishop – which seems rather odd to me and goes against the grain. I suspect many spiritually suitable candidates will never apply in person, though others can put their names forward. But unless you have glowing references as to your track record, gifts and suitability, plus support from members of the Crown Nominations Commission of the General Synod, you won't get very far. Although the process of selection in the Church of England is now much more open than in the past, it is still a far cry from the electioneering and hustings of some parts of the Anglican Communion. I think that it is quite possible to feel that you have something to offer in episcopal ministry and desire to serve God and the Church in that way, yet still shrink from it. I reckon that the combination of willingness and diffidence is healthy. Sometimes prelates are asked, 'Did you want to be bishop/archbishop?' It is unthinkable that the answer could be, 'Yes, I did.' Rowan Williams once replied to that question, 'Not particularly,' which is a beautifully nuanced and ambiguous reply. It is known of some past Archbishops of Canterbury that, as schoolboys, they practised the signature *Cantuar*. Sometimes God winks at youthful pride and emulation.

Throughout the Anglican Communion today bishops are chosen by a process of nomination, election and confirmation – a process that varies in its application from one member Church to another. Anglicans believe that it is right that churches should choose their own bishops and not have them foisted upon them, as they are in some churches. But because a bishop is a bishop in the Church of God, and not only a bishop in a particular diocese or church, the implications of any election for the well-being of the wider Church, and particularly for its unity, should always be taken into account. It is a tremendously affirming experience for bishops to know that they are the Church's choice. But it has not always been the practice for churches to choose their own bishops. Often in history the monarch or equivalent civil ruler had the major or sole say in appointments. In the twentieth century the Roman Catholic Church formalized and bureaucratized the practice of bishops all around the world being appointed by the pope. And until the 1970s British prime ministers had the major responsibility for the appointment of bishops in the Church of England. They simply recommended a name to the Sovereign after consulting the Archbishop of Canterbury and anyone else they thought fit to ask.

It was in that context that Prime Minister William Ewart Gladstone gave a list of qualifications that he looked for in a future bishop. Gladstone had plenty of experience of choosing bishops, being prime minister of the United Kingdom four times. Gladstone was a lay pillar of the Church, a considerable theologian in his own right and more theologically learned than most bishops of his day – and that was saying something![1] Here are his selection criteria:

> Piety, Learning (Sacred), Eloquence, Administrative power. Faithful allegiance to the Church and to the Church of England. Activity. Tact and courtesy in dealings with men, and knowledge of the world. Accomplishments and literature. An equitable spirit. Faculty of working with his brother bishops. Some legal habit of mind. Circumspection. Courage. Maturity of age and character. Corporal

1. For a brief account of Gladstone and the Church see Paul Avis, *Anglicanism and the Christian Church: Theological Resources in Historical Perspective* (2nd edition, London and New York: T&T Clark, 2002), pp. 196–204. The best biography, which does justice to Gladstone's churchmanship, is H. C. G. Matthew, *Gladstone 1809–1898* (Oxford: Clarendon Press, 1997). For studies of Gladstone's religious thought see Perry Butler, *Gladstone: Church, State and Tractarianism* (Oxford: Clarendon Press, 1982) and David Bebbington, *The Mind of Gladstone: Religion, Homer, and Politics* (Oxford: Oxford University Press, 2004).

vigour. Liberal sentiments on public affairs. A representative character with reference to shades of opinion fairly allowable in the Church.[2]

Here we have, rather jumbled up, different kinds of qualities: physical ('vigour'), moral ('circumspection' or discretion; 'courage'), spiritual ('piety', 'faithfulness') and intellectual ('learning', culture). Probably there has never been a bishop who was fully able to meet Gladstone's exacting requirements! As bishops sometimes say to parishes looking for a new rector, 'Only the Archangel Gabriel would match your expectations!'

When Rowan Williams announced his resignation as Archbishop of Canterbury in 2012 he commented wryly that his successor would need the stamina of an ox and the hide of a rhinoceros and many bishops would say 'Amen' to that. But to have a robust constitution and a thick skin simply enables a bishop to survive (which is, after all, the *sine qua non*); it says nothing about the quality or usefulness of that bishop's ministry. What we are attempting to get into focus in this *Theological Handbook of Episcopal Ministry* is precisely the calibre, usefulness and spiritual fruitfulness of the bishop. A 'good-enough' bishop, one who can do the job competently, is something to be thankful for, but perhaps we can set our sights a little higher and ask, 'What makes a really good bishop?' This question is very much in the minds of those who choose a new bishop for the dioceses of the Anglican Communion, through the various methods of nomination, election and confirmation that operate in the member churches.

The same system of episcopal appointment as in Gladstone's day was in place in the Church of England until the early 1970s, when the General Synod was given responsibility for nominating bishops, through the instrumentality of a special commission (now the Crown Nominations Commission), to the prime minister and thence to the Sovereign. In the Church of England the formal stages of Election and Confirmation are still observed, albeit in a rather idiosyncratic way. When these are correctly understood, they can be seen to fulfil a meaningful role.

---

2. Cited (without a reference) by John Morgan in Peter J. Jagger (ed.), *Mr Gladstone: Founder's Day Lectures, St Deiniol's Library, 1931–1955* (St Deiniol's Library, Harwarden, Wales: Monad Press, 2001), p. 185. (St Deiniol's is now renamed 'Gladstone's Library'.)

When Prime Minister Winston Churchill – who was no churchman, in fact no Christian believer – had to find a new Archbishop of Canterbury in the middle of the Second World War, he had no hesitation in proposing William Temple, the Archbishop of York, whom he described as 'the only sixpenny item in a penny bazaar'.[3] Temple was indeed outstanding in several areas: philosopher, theologian, pastor, ecumenist and social prophet. He was the son of an Archbishop of Canterbury, Frederick Temple, whose character as a bishop was described as 'granite on fire'.[4] But Churchill's judgement was unfair to George Bell, Bishop of Chichester, a churchman of great courage and vision, and no intellectual lightweight. But Bell, who had been a vocal critic of the Allies' aerial bombing strategy of Germany, with its huge number of civilian casualties, lacked the ability to project himself on the public stage and was rather deficient in worldly wisdom.[5] Temple's tenure of the See of Canterbury was tragically short (1942–44), but Churchill's choice was abundantly vindicated. This brief scenario from the 1940s is a reminder that church people are not the only ones who evaluate bishops. Bishops have a public profile, a public persona, and their mission is to all who will receive it – especially to 'the lost sheep of the house of Israel'.

A concise summary of what a bishop is was given by Richard Hooker (1554–1600), the prime architect, we might say, of Anglican ecclesiology in the age of Queen Elizabeth I:

A Minister of God, unto whom with permanent continuance, there is given not only power of administering the Word and Sacraments, which power other Presbyters have; but also a

3. On William Temple see F. A. Iremonger, *William Temple, Archbishop of Canterbury: His Life and Letters* (London: Oxford University Press, 1948); John Kent, *William Temple: Church, State and Society in Britain, 1880–1950* (Cambridge: Cambridge University Press, 1992).

4. On Frederick Temple see Peter Hinchliff, *Frederick Temple, Archbishop of Canterbury: A Life* (Oxford: Clarendon Press, 1998).

5. On Bell see R. C. D. Jasper, *George Bell, Bishop of Chichester* (Oxford: Oxford University Press, 1967); Jaakko Rusama, *Unity and Compassion: Moral Issues in the Life and Thought of George K. A. Bell* (Helsinki: The Finnish Society for Missiology and Ecumenics, 1986); Andrew Chandler, *The Church and Humanity: The Life and Work of George Bell, 1883–1958* (Farnham: Ashgate, 2012).

further power to ordain Ecclesiastical persons, and a power of Chiefty in Government over Presbyters as well as Lay men, a power to be by way of jurisdiction a Pastor even unto Pastors themselves.[6]

Hooker has a high view of episcopacy, believing it to be of apostolic institution and divine origin, but he does not regard it as absolutely essential to the existence of the Church. He too is highly exacting in what he expects of bishops. There are some bishops in the English Church, he says, who should never have been let loose on their flock: they are like doctors who learn the art of healing by killing off some of their patients. According to Hooker – and who could disagree with these sentiments? – bishops should be people of learning, of warm devotion and of wise speech. They should be marked by a quality of heart and mind that comes from 'deep meditation of holy things and as it were conversation with God'. They should shine like angels of God in the midst of a perverse generation.[7]

We might profitably compare Richard Hooker's model of episcopal ministry with the way that the bishop's role is described in the Canons of the Churches of the Anglican Communion today. The consensus of the Canons has recently been summarized like this:

> The diocesan bishop has a special responsibility and authority as the chief pastor, minister and teacher of the diocese, a governor and guardian of discipline in the diocese, and exercises ministry in accordance with law.
>
> The bishop as chief pastor must foster the spiritual welfare and unity of the diocese.
>
> The bishop is the principal minister of the word and sacraments, with authority to ensure the worthiness of public worship, and has the right to preside at the eucharist, administer the sacraments, celebrate the rites of ordination and confirmation, preach the word, and perform such other liturgical functions as are prescribed by law.

6. Richard Hooker, *Of the Laws of Ecclesiastical Polity*, VII, 2.2, in Hooker, *Works*, ed. John Keble (Oxford: Oxford University Press, 1845), vol. 3, p. 148.

7. See A. S. McGrade, 'Richard Hooker on Episcopacy and Bishops, Good and Bad', *International Journal for the Study of the Christian Church*, 2.2 (2002), pp. 28–46.

This description of episcopal ministry as it is understood in the Anglican Communion today continues:

> The bishop must teach, uphold and safeguard the faith and doctrine of the church.
>
> The bishop has a role of leadership in the governance of the diocese, is president of the diocesan synod, council or equivalent assembly…
>
> The bishop has a primary responsibility to maintain ecclesiastical discipline in the diocese amongst clergy and laity as required by law.
>
> The bishop must reside in the diocese as required by law.[8]

These characteristics, from a synthesis of Anglican canon law, may seem obvious and uncontroversial, but in fact they comprise a distinctively Anglican understanding of episcopacy, one that is both catholic and reformed. There are churches of other Christian traditions whose bishops do not fit this description in every respect. In some churches bishops do not have effective oversight, but are basically pastors and administrators or chief executives. In other churches there are bishops who have never had a 'see', a bounded portion of the people of God committed to their care. The Anglican concept of a bishop is a lot to expect of anyone!

An account of episcopal ministry that has a considerable weight of ecumenical consensus behind it is that given in the 1982 'Lima' document *Baptism, Eucharist and Ministry*:

> Bishops preach the Word, preside at the sacraments, and administer discipline in such a way as to be representative pastoral ministers of oversight, continuity and unity in the Church. They have pastoral oversight of the area to which they are called. They serve the apostolicity and unity of the Church's teaching, worship and sacramental life. They have responsibility for leadership in the Church's mission. They relate the Christian community in their area to the wider Church, and the universal Church to their community. They, in communion with the presbyters and deacons and the whole

---

8. *The Principles of Canon Law Common to the Churches of the Anglican Communion* (London: Anglican Communion Office, 2008), pp. 47–48: http://www.acclawnet.co.uk/canon-law.php.

community, are responsible for the orderly transfer of ministerial authority in the Church.[9]

Anglican orders

It is not accidental that the set-apart ministries of the Church are termed 'orders'. True order belongs to the nature and mission of the Church. In Christ God has brought a redeemed order into the world. Notwithstanding the glaring fragmentation and appalling dysfunctionality of the Church in many ways, the divine order shines through. Thomas F. Torrance writes: 'Order is the co-ordinating of the life of the Church in its fellowship, worship, and mission in the service of the glory of God … in the new Humanity in Jesus Christ nothing is out of order, or out of proportion. Everything has its proper order, proper time, proper place, proper sequence, and proper end.'[10] The Church conforms to a pattern or shape in time and place, one that is expressed above all in its worship. But, as Torrance reminds us, all order in the historical, visible Church is essentially eschatological; it points to a fulfilment beyond history and is therefore provisional, imperfect and ambiguous.[11] Our place as laity or clergy, even bishops, in the divine ordering of the Church is at the service of a greater end, willed by God. As Andrew Davison puts it, 'The Church is ordered by God as a beginning and instrument for the right ordering of all things.'[12]

The Church is an ordered society, a structured historical community. Although it has been scarred by separation and division, it is called to model order in its own life and to restore God's divine order where that has been lost. 'The Church is intrinsically ordered, and has been from the start.'[13] In its broad contours, the order and ordering of the Church is given. It is not for any single individual

9. *Baptism, Eucharist and Ministry* (Geneva: World Council of Churches, 1982), C 29, pp. 26–27.

10. Thomas F. Torrance, *Conflict and Agreement in the Church, Volume 2: The Ministry and Sacraments of the Gospel* (London: Lutterworth Press, 1960), pp. 13, 15 (first published in *Church Quarterly Review*, CLX (1959), pp. 21–36).

11. Torrance, *Conflict and Agreement in the Church, Volume 2*, p. 18.

12. Andrew Davison, *Why Sacraments?* (London: SPCK, 2013), p. 82.

13. Davison, *Why Sacraments?*, p. 83.

to decide what kind of order best suits God's Church. The orders of ministry – collectively, 'Holy Orders' – reflect and embody the divine order and have the potential to glorify God and bear witness to God's truth. The way that orders of ministry are distributed has a pleasing symmetry and satisfies our love of form. Thomas Aquinas spoke of 'the order of ecclesiastical beauty'.[14]

Bishops of the Anglican Communion are ordained by means of a rite that descends – with revisions, regional variations and a good amount of liturgical creativity – from Archbishop Thomas Cranmer's Ordinal of 1550. This became the basis of the 1662 'classical' Anglican Ordinal which has shaped the understanding of ordained ministry throughout the Anglican Communion (it remains one of the 'historic formularies' of the Church of England). The original Ordinal of 1550 stemmed from a medieval template in the Roman pontificals, adapted in the light of Reformation principles. Influenced by medieval theories, it did not clearly distinguish between priesthood and episcopate, allowing for the possibility that bishops were priests with wider jurisdiction, rather than a separate order. That is what explains why, in the first English Prayer Books, bishops are said to be 'consecrated', rather than ordained. That language soon seemed inadequate; the blurring of priesthood and episcopate is unhelpful when we need clarity about the various callings and offices in the Church. Bishops are, of course, priests – they are deacons too – but they are not simply priests who have been given extra responsibility, more work to do. They belong to a third order of ministry, the episcopate. The distinctiveness of the episcopate as an order was emphasized by the Second Vatican Council, which ascribed to it the 'fullness' of the three orders because it includes – and transcends – the orders of diaconate and presbyterate.[15] However, it remains true that bishops, like all clergy, are 'consecrated' in the sense that they are marked out and set apart for a divine calling. Cranmer's Ordinal, which had undergone significant modification in 1552 in a more Protestant direction, was revised in 1662 in a slightly more catholic direction, following the restoration of the monarchy in the person of Charles II, and with it the episcopal form of the Church of England. In 1662 the orders were clearly distinguished, and the language was strengthened while still remaining somewhat equivocal: bishops were said be 'ordained

14. Aquinas, *Summa Theologiae*, II-II, Qn 183, Art 3, *Resp.*
15. *Lumen Gentium*, §21.

or consecrated'.[16] Some modern Anglican ordinals use the expression 'consecration and ordination' (e.g. The Church in the Province of the West Indies) or 'ordination and consecration' (e.g. the Church of England). The Episcopal Church, in its 1979 *Book of Common Prayer*, uses simply 'Ordination' in the title of the rite, but slips 'consecrate' into the text. In modern Anglicanism, with one or two exceptions, 'consecrate' has become assimilated to 'ordain' and in fact the latter term would be theologically correct and sufficient on its own.

The Churches of the Anglican Communion uphold the historic threefold ministry and normally permit only those who have received episcopal ordination, within the historic succession, to be appointed to a clerical office. The Preface to the 1550 Ordinal (repeated in the 1662 revision) makes the dubious claim that the orders of bishops, priests and deacons have existed 'from the Apostles tyme' (sic).[17] Modern scholarship does not support this bold assertion, though it could certainly be argued that the generally charismatic, largely pragmatic ministries that we find in the New Testament foreshadow later developments and that the threefold ministry has evolved from those earlier more inchoate forms. The office of bishop, together with that of presbyter and deacon, is first clearly seen in the Letters of St Ignatius, Bishop of Antioch, early in the second century.[18] But the bishops referred to in the Ignatian letters could not have come out of the blue and would not have been invented by Ignatius himself.

16. The indispensable study is Paul Bradshaw, *The Anglican Ordinal: Its History and Development from the Reformation to the Present Day* (London: SPCK/Alcuin Club, 1971). The definitive text is in F. E. Brightman, *The English Rite*, 2 vols (2nd edition, London: Rivingtons, 1921; republished Farnborough, Hants: Gregg, 1970), vol. 1, pp. cxxx–cxli; vol. 2, pp. 928–1017. An excellent broad survey is Paul Bradshaw, *Rites of Ordination: Their History and Theology* (London: SPCK, 2014). A shorter synopsis is C. Jones, G. Wainwright, E. Yarnold and P. Bradshaw (eds), *The Study of Liturgy* (2nd edition, London: SPCK, 1992), chapter 6. A useful short discussion is Bryan D. Spinks and Gianfranco Tellini, 'The Anglican Church and Holy Order', in Kenneth Stevenson and Bryan D. Spinks (eds), *The Identity of Anglican Worship* (London: Mowbray, 1991), chapter 10.

17. *The First and Second Prayer Books of King Edward VI* (London: Dent; New York: Dutton, 1910), p. 292.

18. See, e.g., *Early Christian Writings*, trans. Maxwell Staniforth (Harmondsworth: Penguin, 1968).

As Nicholas Afanasiev puts it, 'The ecclesial mind would not have accepted what did not exist previously.'[19] These bishops emerged in history as the result of development – though whether they derived by delegation from the apostles or emerged from the presbyterate is a matter of debate.

The fact that the pattern of deacon, priest and bishop did not become universal until the early fourth century certainly does not mean that the threefold ministry that Anglicans uphold rests on a shaky foundation. The threefold ministry emerged as the Church took permanent shape in history, along with the Canon of Scripture, the ecumenical Creeds, the shape of the Eucharist and the need to reach a *modus vivendi*, a constructive relationship with the state, as far as possible (more on this point later). As Davison points out, the pattern of ministry and sacramental order that came to be characteristic of the Church had become established well before other matters, matters that today we regard as inviolable, were settled, notably the doctrine of Christ's human and divine natures and the doctrine of the Trinity.[20]

Modern Anglican liturgies make more modest claims for the antiquity of their orders. The Church of England's *Common Worship Ordinal* merely states, 'The Church of England maintains the historic threefold ministry of bishops, priests and deacons. Its ministers are ordained by bishops according to authorized forms of service, with prayer and the laying on of hands ...'. *A New Zealand Prayer Book* is laconic: 'Within the ordained ministry there are three orders: deacons, priests (also called presbyters) and bishops.' Rather surprisingly, the *Book of Common Prayer* (1979) of The Episcopal Church repeats Cranmer's claim for the New Testament origin of the three orders in its own words, but interestingly it elsewhere lists 'lay persons' among the 'orders' of the Church ('Concerning the Service of the Church').

The ordination liturgies of the Anglican Church in Aotearoa, New Zealand and Polynesia, the Scottish Episcopal Church and the Church of England, to take three examples that are to hand, each provides a brief but powerful theology of Christian ministry as the framework for

19. Nicholas Afanasiev, *The Church of the Holy Spirit*, trans. Vitaly Permiakov; ed. and intro. Michael Plekon; Foreword Rowan Williams (Notre Dame, IN: University of Notre Dame Press, 2007), p. 217.

20. Davison, *Why Sacraments?*, p. 90. See also John Macquarrie, *A Guide to the Sacraments* (London: SCM Press, 1997), pp. 194–196.

ordination. They make it clear that the Church is a communion, one body, that all Christians share in the priesthood of Christ, that all are called to ministry in baptism, a call that is constantly renewed in the Eucharist, and that the ordained are set apart to promote and support the ministry of the whole Church.[21]

Modern ordination rites have replaced Cranmer's imperative formulae, 'Take thou authority…' and 'Receive the Holy Ghost…', with the invocation in prayer of the Holy Spirit for the needed gifts of ministry. Such invocation of the Spirit acknowledges the vital truth that ordination comes from God, albeit through human instrumentality. A liturgy of holy order that spells out that ordination is the calling and gift of the sovereign Holy Spirit puts the emphasis where it rightly belongs – with God not with humans. It also sets human authority and ecclesiastical hierarchy in perspective. Moreover, it is conducive to modesty *vis-à-vis* other churches – ecumenical humility – and helps to pave the way for a greater recognition of the authenticity of the ministries of other, non-episcopal churches than has been usual in ecumenical dialogue involving Anglicans.

The invocation of the Holy Spirit – the *epiclesis* – is expressed particularly strongly and vividly in *A New Zealand Prayer Book*. Before the actual ordination the Spirit is solemnly invoked:

Holy Spirit of God,
meet us in this moment
as you met the apostles of old.
Be with us, Holy Spirit,
[the people respond] bring faith and hope, we pray.

Then, as the presiding bishop and other bishops lay hands on the head of the bishop-elect, the presiding bishop says:

God of grace, through your Holy Spirit,
gentle as a dove, living, burning as fire,

21. See the discussion in Charles Hefling and Cynthia Shattuck (eds), *The Oxford Guide to the Book of Common Prayer: A Worldwide Survey* (Oxford: Oxford University Press, 2006), pp. 421–423. For an exposition of similar, though not identical, principles see Paul Avis, *A Ministry Shaped by Mission* (London and New York: T&T Clark, 2005).

empower your servant *N*
for the office and work
of a bishop in the Church.

Some Anglican clergy have been troubled – and some still are – by
the fact that the Roman Catholic Church does not recognize their holy
orders as valid, that in fact it formally and definitively condemned them
('absolutely null and utterly void') in Pope Leo XIII's Bull *Apostolicae
Curae* (1896). The official, historic Roman Catholic position is that
Anglican clergy are lay people masquerading as priests and bishops.
Although to be a member of the lay faithful, the baptized people of God,
is an exalted calling, Anglicans have consistently repudiated the Roman
Catholic judgement on their ordinations and their celebrations of the
Eucharist. Although Rome's historic hostile stance has been modified
in practice by various warm gestures of tacit recognition on the part
of recent popes (notably Paul VI giving Michael Ramsey his episcopal
ring), the fact remains that Anglicans wishing to exercise their ministry
within the Roman Catholic Church are required to be (re-)ordained
and – particularly galling – Roman Catholics are not officially permitted,
under any circumstances, to receive Holy Communion at an Anglican
celebration of the Eucharist. So it is good for Anglican clergy – especially
bishops – to be aware that *Apostolicae Curae* (1896) was comprehensively,
indeed crushingly, refuted at the time by the Archbishops of Canterbury
and York, with the aid of the most learned bishops of the Church of
England, in their response *Saepius Officio*.[22] Anglican clergy can be
confident that their orders are secure, that they are catholic and apostolic
and are authentic ministries of the one Church of Jesus Christ.

The good-enough bishop

In getting to the heart of episcopal ministry as Anglicans understand
it, the Anglican canons and liturgies certainly help. But before going

22. See the discussion in Paul Avis, *The Identity of Anglicanism: Essentials of
Anglican Identity* (London and New York, T&T Clark, 2008), chapter 8: 'Anglican
Orders: From *Apostolicae Curae* to Women Bishops', which also provides a basic
bibliography. See especially C. Hill and E. Yarnold (eds), *Anglican Orders: The
Documents in the Debate* (Norwich: Canterbury Press, 1997). The background
to *Apostolicae Curae* is given in Viscount Halifax, *Leo XIII and Anglican Orders*
(London: Longmans, Green, and Co., 1912).

any further, it is important to bear in mind that many aspects of episcopal ministry are not exclusive to bishops: they are either shared with the whole Church, or with all the ordained, and are exercised in a collegial and/or communal context (see the discussion of these aspects below). While there are some differences of role as well as of style in the practice of bishops throughout the Anglican Communion, the theology of what a bishop is and does is essentially the same. We can say that, in the Anglican understanding of episcopacy, the identity of a bishop in the Church of God is made up of a number of facets or complementary aspects. When they are brought together in one person, they result in a highly significant ministerial office in the Christian Church. The ministry of a bishop is therefore regarded by all Anglicans as of vital importance for the unity and continuity of the Church, and for its mission. Our ecumenical partners among the non-episcopal churches are sometimes bemused or exasperated by the fact that Anglicans are wedded to episcopacy, that Anglicans love their bishops, even if that love is often somewhat ambivalent. But certainly, the visible historical continuity of holy orders, embodied in the historic episcopate, is an identifying mark of Anglicanism throughout the world.

A good-enough bishop is a precious gift of God to God's Church. While it is true that some dioceses revive after the bishop has moved on – just as some parishes spring back to life after the departure of their priest, whose presence acted like a wet blanket on lay initiative – a good bishop is a source of strength, inspiration and wisdom to his or her people. Bishops can make a qualitative difference, for good or ill, to how church people experience their faith, worship and witness from day to day. How Christian people see their bishop affects their morale – for better or worse. Bishops set the overall tone of their dioceses by their example, their words and their actions. But a poorly equipped bishop – one who lacks understanding of the office or the skills and aptitudes to carry it out – is a serious liability. A bishop who is not up to the job can have a devastating effect on the morale and functioning of the diocese and hold back its mission.

A bishop is entrusted with a daunting role and is asked to do an extremely difficult job. Some clergy crave a bishopric and think that somehow they deserve it, but if they get it, they find it is not quite what they hoped for. There is always a sense that a prospective bishop should shrink from the responsibilities that will be thrust upon him or her. There is an ancient tradition of reluctance: the candidate would decline twice over, sincerely or in pretence, with the words, *Nolo episcopari* ('I do not want to be a bishop').[23] Some would say that a bishop has a thankless task. But a bishop is not a bishop in order to be thanked. A bishop's first thought will be, in the words of St Paul, 'Who is sufficient for these things?' Lancelot Andrewes, an eminent scholarly bishop in early seventeenth-century England, had those words engraved on his episcopal seal. But a bishop will answer that question in the same way that St Paul does: 'Our sufficiency is of God' (2 Corinthians 2.16; 3.5, KJB).

The bishop's first priority in fulfilling the role that is thrust upon him or her is not to ask, 'How well am I doing?' or, 'How am I going down with my people?', but to be faithful to the calling that they have received from God and the Church. If a bishop's aim in life is to please the people and to be a popular figure that everyone loves, she/he will be a dismal failure as a bishop. A bishop seeking popularity is doomed to fail; their integrity is already draining away. 'Woe to you when all speak well of you, for that is what their ancestors did to the false prophets' (Luke 6.26). As Abraham Lincoln famously said, 'You can please all of the people some of the time, some of the people all of the time, but you can never please all of the people all of the time.'

But what is the bishop's calling? What is a bishop? Where is episcopal identity to be located? The bishop's identity – the nature of his or her ministry and office – is something that is *received*. It is received from the Church, or rather from the Holy Spirit, not created by the individual bishop. It is given in ordination by the Spirit through the Church by means of prayer with the laying on of the hands of the bishops, those who are already placed within the historic episcopate. Just as we cannot baptize ourselves, but receive baptism from God through the Holy Spirit, so we cannot ordain ourselves, but receive ordination from God through the Church. St Paul asks the Corinthians, 'What do you have that you did not receive?' (1 Corinthians 4.7). 'From his fullness we have all received, grace upon grace' (John 1.16).

In the Anglican Communion there is a continuous succession of bishops, going back to the apostolic age, which is one of the ways (though not necessarily the most important) in which we know that the Church of today is the same Church as the Church of the apostles – that the Church is apostolic. It is clear from the study of Church history that

23. See the rogues gallery at https://www.google.com/search?hl=en&safe= active&biw=1243&bih=904&gbv=2&tbm=isch&sa=1&q=nolo+episcopari&aq =f&aqi=g10&aql=&oq=

the Anglican understanding of episcopacy and its practice has evolved considerably over the centuries, as it has in the Roman Catholic Church. However, there is a strong case for thinking that the essentials have remained much the same over time, while the emphasis on different aspects of episcopal ministry has varied. Anglicans look not only to Scripture, but also to patristic and medieval, as well as to Reformation and modern models, of episcopacy as sources for how they understand that ministry now. What then is a bishop?

Chapter 2

THE BISHOP'S IDENTITY AND TASKS

So, what is a bishop?[1] In 1924, when he was Archbishop of York, Cosmo Gordon Lang sat for his portrait by Sir William Orpen. It is said that, when the portrait was shown to some bishops of the Church of England, Lang complained, 'They say in that portrait I look proud, prelatical and pompous.' Hensley Henson, Bishop of Durham, interjected, 'And may I ask Your Grace to which of these epithets Your Grace takes exception?' Henson's typically waspish comment was unfair to Lang whose shy and introspective nature could make him seem aloof.[2] Proud prelacy is almost entirely a thing of the past, at least in Anglicanism, but it still tinges the image of bishops held by Christians from non-episcopal churches. The antidote to any suspicion of prelacy is to answer our question, 'What is a bishop?', by beginning with what a bishop has in common with all Christians.

Baptized disciple of Jesus Christ

First things first: at bottom a bishop is a baptized disciple of Christ. This is surely the right place to start, the bottom line of Christian identity. Before we say to ourselves, 'I'm a bishop,' we must say, 'I am a disciple of Jesus Christ, baptised into union with his death and resurrection.' Before they could be apostles, the twelve had to be disciples, keeping

1. The following description follows the outline that I drafted for the report, *Embracing the Covenant: Quinquennial Report of the Joint Implementation Commission under the Covenant between The Methodist Church of Great Britain and The Church of England* (Peterborough: Methodist Publishing House, 2008), pp. 91–95.

2. J. G. Lockhart, *Cosmo Gordon Lang* (London: Hodder and Stoughton, 1949), p. 290; Owen Chadwick, *Hensley Henson: A Study in the Friction between Church and State* (Oxford: Oxford University Press, 1983), p. 244.

company with Jesus and learning of him through his words and deeds (Mark 3.14). In a sense they remained disciples all their lives, taught by the Spirit of Christ to conform their lives to his, marked with the character of Christ. As his lifelong disciples today, we are sacramentally united with our teacher. Luther said that when the devil threatened or temptations approached, he would declare, 'I am baptised!' Therefore nothing could separate him from the love of Christ (Romans 8.35). Or as St Augustine said to his people, 'With you I am a Christian; for you I am a bishop.' A bishop is first of all a member of the *laos*, the people of God. Like all Christians, the bishop has been incorporated into the body of Christ in baptism through the power of the Holy Spirit (1 Corinthians 12.13). All the faithful are loved equally by God, equally dear to God. A bishop is not nearer to God or more important in God's sight than any other Christian. In the Kingdom of God 'some are last who will be first, and some are first who will be last' (Luke 13.30). Baptism is the deepest foundation of all Christian ministry and those who minister never cease to be disciples, continually instructed in the school of Christ.

Deacon

A bishop is a deacon, called to serve God and God's Church. Like the Roman Catholic and Orthodox Churches, Anglican Churches practise sequential (or cumulative) ordination: deacon–priest–bishop. A priest does not cease to be a deacon and a bishop does not cease to be a priest and a deacon. The character of an order, once given, remains.[3] So it is rather important to know what a deacon is. In classical and New Testament Greek, the word *diakonia*, from which we get our word 'diaconate', is a secular term denoting commissioned agency and a *diakonos* is a person who is entrusted with a task by someone in authority.[4] So we may say that a deacon receives the fundamental commission of Christ to his Church (Matthew

3. Cf. Church of England Canon C 1.2.
4. John N. Collins, *Diakonia: Reinterpreting the Ancient Sources* (Oxford: Oxford University Press, 1990); John N. Collins, *Deacons and the Church* (Leominster: Gracewing; Harrisburg: Morehouse, 2002); John N. Collins, *Diakonal Studies* (New York: Oxford University Press, 2014); Paul Avis, *A Ministry Shaped by Mission* (London and New York: T&T Clark, 2005).

28.16–20), a commission that is expressed in that particular form of the ministry (*diakonia*) of word, sacrament and pastoral care that is appropriate to a deacon. In other words, deacons are entrusted with a share in the Church's mission. In Anglicanism, as in most Christian traditions, deacons do not have oversight in the community or preside in the celebration of the sacraments, but they assist priests and bishops who do. If *diakonia* is a fundamentally responsible agency on behalf of someone in authority, all Christians are 'under authority' (cf. Matthew 8.9) and the diaconate, in which bishops share, is a reminder, a sign of that truth. In the Acts of the Apostles (Acts 1.25; 6.4) and the Epistles of St Paul *diakonia/diakonos* often has a missionary or apostolic thrust; Paul speaks of the *diakonia* that has been entrusted to him to make the revelation of God in Jesus Christ known to all (2 Corinthians 5.18; Ephesians 3.7). To be a deacon is to have received the fundamental commission, given by Christ to his Church, to make him known in word and deed through the gospel.

Presbyter

'Presbyter' (*presbuteros*) is the New Testament word for 'elder' (e.g. Acts 11.30; 14.23; 20.17; 1 Timothy 4.14; 5.1, 17, 19; Titus 1.5; James 5.14). 'Priest', the term retained in Thomas Cranmer's Ordinal (1550), is derived from it. According to the doctrine of sequential ordination that is inscribed in Anglican formularies, a bishop remains a priest. As Michael Ramsey puts it, 'The bishop is still a priest, and unless he retains the heart and mind of a priest he will be a bad bishop.'[5] Priesthood is fundamental to episcopal ministry because priesthood is essentially concerned with the worship of God, the celebration of the sacraments and the reconciliation of God's people to God and to one another. All baptized persons share in the royal, prophetic priesthood of Jesus Christ, given to his Church (1 Peter 2.4–10). Therefore, a priest is a member of the royal prophetic priesthood who has also received the sacramental sign of the ministry of reconciliation through ordination (cf. 2 Corinthians 5.18–20). A priest is commissioned to preach and teach, to preside at the celebration of the sacraments and to exercise

5. Ramsey, *The Christian Priest Today* (revised edition, London: SPCK, 1985), p. 96.

pastoral oversight in collaboration with others. Because the order of bishop includes and embraces, so to speak, the orders of deacon and priest, episcopacy can be seen as the most fully representative ministry of the Church.

Chief pastor

A bishop is the senior pastor or shepherd of the portion of the people of God committed to his or her care: 'the chief pastor of all that are within his diocese, as well laity as clergy, and their father in God'.[6] Anglicans can endorse what the Second Vatican Council said about the pastoral role of the bishop within the diocese:

> A diocese is a portion of the people of God which is entrusted to a bishop to be shepherded by him with the cooperation of the presbytery. Thus by adhering to its pastor and gathered together by him through the Gospel and the Eucharist in the Holy Spirit, it constitutes a particular church in which the one, holy, catholic, and apostolic Church of Christ is truly present and operative.[7]

A bishop is essentially a pastor, rather than a chief executive officer (CEO). Bishops struggle against being sucked into a CEO role. Perhaps some do not struggle quite hard enough. True, the bishop needs an understanding of managerial and executive functions, which are unquestionably vital to the success of an organization, but that does not necessarily mean that the bishop needs to manage in person. To some extent, these functions can be carried out on the bishop's behalf by suitably gifted and trained lay staff persons. What we need to keep in our sights above all is the theological truth that bishops are first and last the chief pastors within the Christian community. The bishop remains a priest among priests and a pastor among pastors (1 Peter 5.1–2). As we shall see in more depth later, the collegial or collaborative dimension of episcopal ministry, both with fellow bishops in the episcopal college and with priests of the diocese, is pivotal. The Church of England's *Common Worship Ordinal*

---

6. Church of England Canon C 18.

7. *Christus Dominus*, §11: http://www.ewtn.com/library/councils/v2bishop .htm.

says of bishops, 'As chief pastors, it is their duty to share with their fellow presbyters the oversight of the Church.' The Book of Common Prayer of The Episcopal Church (and that of The Church in the Province of the West Indies) asks candidate bishops, 'Will you sustain your fellow presbyters and take counsel with them … ?' It is from the responsibility of oversight that the bishop's ministry of word and sacrament flows. As Paul Bradshaw has written, ' … it is because they [bishops] preside over the Christian community that they preside over its worship (and not the other way round), and because they have the responsibility to preserve the community in truth that they are its principal ministers of the word.'[8]

Minister of word and sacrament

The Church can be described ecclesiologically as the community where the ministry of word and sacrament take place in the name of Jesus Christ, in the context of pastoral care. A church can be identified by the signs of word and sacrament, faithfully performed. For the sixteenth-century Reformers, the ministry of word and sacrament were the marks (*notae*) of where the true Church was to be found. As the Thirty-Nine Articles puts it, 'The visible Church of Christ is a congregation of faithful men, in the which the pure Word of God is preached, and the Sacraments be duly ministered according to Christ's ordinance in all those things that of necessity are requisite to the same.'[9] If word and sacrament are indicative of the Church, and indeed constitutive of it, it follows that a bishop's primary tasks are to proclaim the gospel and to celebrate the sacraments of the gospel. Bishops are 'principal ministers of word and sacrament' among the portion of the people of God committed to their care.[10] Some

8. Paul Bradshaw, 'Ordination as God's Action through the Church', in David R. Holeton (ed.), *Anglican Orders and Ordinations* (Cambridge: Grove Books, 1997), pp. 8–15, at p. 13.

9. Thirty-Nine Articles of Religion, Article XIX. N.B. 'Congregation' of the faithful (*coetus fidelium*) does not have its modern meaning of a local group of worshippers; in the sixteenth century it had a national and even universal reference.

10. *Common Worship Ordinal*; cf. Church of England Canon C 18. 4.

misplaced suspicions of Anglican 'prelacy', on the part of members of non-episcopal churches, can be allayed when they see for themselves that Anglican bishops are primarily devoted to the ministry of the word (preaching and teaching) and to presiding at and overseeing the celebration of the sacraments, and that bishops surround these tasks with a deeply personal ministry of pastoral care. In these ways, the ministry of bishops actually spearheads the mission of the Church, which is neither more nor less than proclaiming Christ through word, sacrament and pastoral care in all its many practical forms.

Overseer (episkopos)

Bishops have a crucial role in the governance of the Church. *Episkopos* in the Greek New Testament is literally one who oversees. 'Keep watch over yourselves and over all the flock, of which the Holy Spirit has made you overseers, to shepherd the church of God that he obtained by the blood of his own Son' (Acts 20.28). By virtue of their ordination, bishops have the responsibility of oversight within their diocese and, collectively with other bishops, throughout their church, including a special responsibility for its doctrine, worship and ministry. 'To govern' is the third of the widely recognized tasks (*munera*), given by Christ to the Church and its ministers, after 'to teach' and 'to sanctify'. A bishop's oversight is exercised in personal, collegial and communal ways (see further below). Collaboration is facilitated through synodical structures, including the diocesan synod and the bishop's council or an equivalent body. 'The bishop in synod' is the phrase that captures the nature of oversight in Anglicanism. Advised by legal experts, the bishop administers the law of the church and the clergy are pledged to 'canonical obedience'. The *Common Worship Ordinal* puts it like this: 'As chief pastors, it is their duty to share with their fellow presbyters the oversight of the Church, speaking in the name of God and expounding the gospel of salvation. With the Shepherd's love, they are to be merciful, but with firmness; to minister discipline, but with compassion.'[11] All of a bishop's functions, including confirmation and ordination, derive from the fact that the bishop is ordained to oversight, to responsible care of all that goes on in the portion of the people of God committed to that bishop and in certain respects, more widely.

11. *Common Worship Ordinal.*

Guardian of true doctrine

As a guardian of the apostolic faith, a bishop carries out this responsibility by teaching, preaching and (on advice) administering discipline. 'It appertains to his office to teach and to uphold sound and wholesome doctrine, and to banish and drive away all erroneous and strange opinions.'[12] Of course, the whole priesthood shares this responsibility, as do all Christians: the faithful have their share in the faith that is entrusted to the whole Church and is apprehended through the *sensus fidelium*, the instinct that the faithful have for the truth of God.[13] The bishop is the servant of the Church's faith. His or her personal theological views should remain in the background. The bishop is essentially an exponent of the faith of the Church through the ages. While much in Christian belief changes or varies from century to century and from culture to culture, the credal core of the faith remains constant. Like the Apostle Paul, the bishop passes on what she/he has received (1 Corinthians 11.2, 23; 15.1–3), articulating it in a way that is both faithful and attractive. A bishop's personal opinions, quirky ideas or theological hobby-horses are not relevant to the exercise of the office. As Michael Ramsey commented, the bishop 'will know enough history to avoid facile enthusiasm for novelties for their own sake, and enough of the deeper things of theology to distinguish what is shallow and superficial from what is likely to be lasting. As the keeper of the tradition of Christ he will know what are the things which are not shaken'.[14] In view of the militant challenges to faith in this secular yet credulous age, I would expect a bishop to be a competent Christian apologist, able to offer in the public forum a convincing and attractive account of Christian belief, 'a defence ... of the hope that is in [us]' (1 Peter 3.15). Whether a bishop can be a theological explorer, as well as a faithful teacher, working on the boundary as well as at the centre, is a question that we will consider later.

12. Church of England Canon C 18. 1.

13. On the *sensus fidei*, etc., see the report of the Roman Catholic International Theological Commission, *Sensus Fidei in the Life of the Church* (2014): http://www.vatican.va/roman_curia/congregations/cfaith/cti_documents/rc_cti_20140610_sensus-fidei_en.html

14. Ramsey, *The Christian Priest Today*, p. 98.

Successor of the apostles

Bishops are regarded in Anglican, as well as in Orthodox and Roman Catholic ecclesiology, as successors of the twelve apostles. This looks like an extremely grandiose claim and one that raises expectations that cannot be realized – including that bishops should be able to work miracles! So what does it mean? Obviously, bishops cannot be successors of the apostles in respect of the apostles' unique, irreplaceable role as witnesses to Christ's resurrection (Luke 24.48; Acts 1.8). What is meant, I suggest, is that bishops continue the work of the apostles in three ways: (a) upholding, expounding and promoting the apostolic faith; (b) leading the faithful in the apostolic mission of the gospel in the midst of the world; and (c) being a visible link through history, by continuous succession, with the Church of the apostles. In these three ways, the episcopate – the historic episcopate – forms one of the building blocks of the visible, faithful continuity of the Church through history, that is to say, its apostolicity. As Michael Ramsey succinctly puts it with reference to the early Church, 'The Episcopate succeeded the Apostolate as the organ of unity and continuity.'[15] Here Ramsey was making an ecclesiological, rather than an historical statement. It is clear that by the end of the second century the apostolic functions of maintaining unity and continuity, as well as that of oversight, had passed to the office of bishop. But the extent of the transfer of functions and the way that it happened remain matters of debate, even of speculation.[16]

The Gospels speak of the twelve apostles, but there were other apostles, beyond the twelve, including Paul, and twelve may be a stereotyped number to conform to the twelve tribes of Israel. Not only are there, in the New Testament, more than twelve apostles, but there are different understandings of what an apostle is (Barrett finds eight). Contrary to popular assumption, it seems that the twelve were not

---

15. A. M. Ramsey, *The Gospel and the Catholic Church* (London: Longmans, Green & Co., 1936), p. 223.

16. See Raymond E. Brown, *Priest and Bishop: Biblical Reflections* (London: Geoffrey Chapman, 1971); C. K. Barrett, *The Signs of an Apostle: The Cato Lecture 1969* (2nd edition, Carlisle: Paternoster Press, 1996 [1st edition, London: Epworth Press, 1970]); Francis A. Sullivan, S.J., *From Apostles to Bishops: The Development of the Episcopacy in the Early Church* (New York and Mahwah, NJ: The Newman Press, 2001); Alistair C. Stewart, *The Original Bishops: Office and Order in the First Christian Communities* (Grand Rapids, MI: Baker Academic, 2014).

missionaries who travelled to the ends of the earth with the gospel. They seem to have been based, at least at first, in Jerusalem and the surrounding area (Acts 8.1; 11.1; 12.3; 15.4). Neither did they preside as resident chief pastors in a local church – not even in Jerusalem, where James (not the apostle but the brother of the Lord) appears to have had a presiding role (Acts 15.13–21). It was Paul who was the missionary apostle who founded churches and continued, even when not physically present, to have oversight of them. And it is Paul's concept of an apostle as a missionary and founder of churches that has become the normative understanding of apostolic ministry. But, as an outsider, Paul had to seek approval from the apostles and elders in Jerusalem for his mission to the Gentiles and his gospel of radical freedom from the law. The apostles were not a loose bunch of freelance individuals, each doing his own thing as he thought fit, but were constituted as a body, a team, a unit, possibly a council – or in later ecclesiology, a 'college' – by the call and commission of Christ (Mark 3.13–19; Matthew 28.16–20). Collectively the apostles were responsible for the welfare and integrity of the Church – and in that sense bishops follow in their footsteps.

To affirm the apostolic character of episcopal ministry is not a purely 'catholic' or 'high church' idea. It was held by Thomas Cranmer and is reflected in the classical Anglican Ordinal of 1662. The ordinal connects bishops to the apostles in this slightly oblique way, characteristic of the collect form: 'Almighty God, who by thy Son Jesus Christ didst give to thy holy Apostles many excellent gifts, and didst charge them to feed thy flock: give grace, we beseech thee, to all bishops, the Pastors of thy Church ... .' When bishops lay on hands in the 1662 'Order of Confirmation', they do so 'after the example of thy holy Apostles'. Anglicans can endorse what Vatican II says on this point: 'As legitimate successors of the Apostles and members of the episcopal college, bishops should realize that they are bound together and should manifest a concern for all the churches. For by divine institution and the rule of the apostolic office each one together with all the other bishops is responsible for the Church.'[17]

The process of transition from apostle to bishop in the early Church remains obscure, but, as the Anglican-Orthodox report *The Church of the Triune God* puts it: 'Historically it is safe to conclude that the apostles did not hand on a fixed ministerial structure to a college

17. *Christus Dominus*, §6: http://www.ewtn.com/library/councils/v2bishop
.htm; cf. *Lumen Gentium*, §20–21.

of bishops as part of a clearly-defined threefold order of bishops, presbyters and deacons. The picture is one of gradual development from various forms of *episcope* always present, into a pattern of one bishop in each local church…'[18] Francis Sullivan, S.J., suggests that there were probably two streams of transmission from apostle to bishop: (a) by delegation through the co-workers of the apostles, including the apostolic delegates such as Timothy and Titus; and (b) by elevation from the local church leaders, *presbuteroi/episkopoi*, such as those mentioned in Philippians 1.1 and Acts 20.1, 28.[19] Altogether, while there is not a single New Testament example of apostles laying hands on bishops, a sound theological case can be made for holding, as Anglicans do, that bishops are successors of the apostles in certain defined ways. This further suggests that the episcopate belongs to God's intention for the Church, that it is, albeit through a process of providential development, of divine institution. However, that is not the same as saying that episcopacy is of the *esse* of the Church, such that no church can be a church without it. That has always been very much a minority view among Anglican theologians, has not been officially endorsed and has not figured in Anglican ecumenical dialogue.

Leader in mission

Part of the bishop's calling, as recent Lambeth Conferences have stressed, is to lead the church in mission, including evangelization, within the diocese. Bishops are representatives of the Church when they do what the Church does – and, as Emil Brunner once said, the Church exists by mission as a fire exists by burning. So bishops are most truly at the heart of the Church when they are leading their people in mission – that is to say essentially, reaching out in intelligent, credible persuasive ways to those who are not yet within the fold. They do this in person primarily through proclaiming the gospel, showing the way to personal faith and promoting the sacramental path of Christian initiation.[20]

18. *The Church of the Triune God: The Cyprus Agreed Statement of the International Commission for Anglican-Orthodox Theological Dialogue 2006* (London: Anglican Communion Office, 2006), V. 4, p. 60.

19. Sullivan, *From Apostles to Bishops*, p. 223.

20. See Paul Avis (ed.), *The Journey of Christian Initiation: Theological and Pastoral Perspectives* (London: Church House Publishing, 2011).

In the Anglican Church of Aotearoa, New Zealand and Polynesia the candidate bishop promises to 'promote the unity and mission for which Christ prayed'. In the Church of England bishops are asked, 'Will you lead your people in proclaiming the glorious gospel of Christ, so that the good news of salvation may be heard in every place?' But bishops also carry out their missiological task when they encourage, guide, enable and oversee the outreach of parishes and congregations in their local contexts. Example, teaching and guidance in policy are key modes of the bishop in mission. It is certainly desirable that every bishop should be capable of speaking publicly about the basic truths of the Christian faith, but the least that bishops can do is to sponsor and support public teaching, in the form of lectures, courses or seminars – including opportunities for questions, dialogue and discussion – on Christian beliefs, introduction to the Bible and basic theology, by those best qualified to give these. In the western and westernized world, at least, apologetics is now at the cutting edge of mission and bishops need actively to sponsor and promote it.

Focus and sign of unity

A bishop is entrusted with a special responsibility with regard to the visible unity of the body of Christ. The bishop's unity role takes effect not only within the diocese, but also between dioceses and between the Church of the present and the Church of the past and the Church of the future. The bishop is both a focus and a sign of the unity of the Church. First, the bishop is a *focus* of unity, the central point at which issues of unity converge, the place of intensity with regard to unity matters in a diocese and, collectively, in a church. The bishop is also a *sign* of unity: through his or her visible continuity with the Church of the Apostles in the apostolic succession the bishop represents and manifests the unity that is an indestructible facet of Christ's Church. The bishop's role as both focus and sign of unity is vividly displayed in the ordination of a new bishop. As the Anglican Roman-Catholic International Commission (ARCIC) puts it in its report 'Ministry and Ordination' (1973):

> In the ordination of a new bishop, other bishops lay hands on him, as they request the gift of the Spirit for his ministry and receive him into their ministerial fellowship. Because they are entrusted with the oversight of other churches, this participation in his ordination

signifies that the new bishop and his church are within the communion of churches. Moreover, because they are representative of their churches in fidelity to the teaching and ministry of the apostles and are members of the episcopal college, their participation also ensures the historical continuity of this church with the apostolic Church and of its bishop with the original apostolic ministry.

ARCIC concluded: 'The communion of the churches in mission, faith, and holiness, through time and space, is thus symbolized and maintained in the bishop.'[21]

The office of bishop is an effective sign and instrument of this visible continuity across space and time. The bishop leads the church not only in mission, but in unity, and this makes theological sense because in the New Testament there is an indissoluble connection between the two.[22] Mission and unity are the twin imperatives for all of us who are passionately concerned that the Church should be the *Church*, that its true, God-given nature should shine out. At their ordination new bishops for the Church of England are asked: 'Will you promote peace and reconciliation in the Church and in the world; and will you strive for the visible unity of Christ's Church?' (*Common Worship Ordinal*). A bishop can be an effective focus of unity as a reconciler, promoting deeper mutual understanding between persons in a state of alienation or conflict (using professional mediators where appropriate). This makes the bishop a leader in ecumenism – that is to say, someone with a passion for the visible unity of the Church, an example of courtesy, friendship and co-operation with regard to fellow church leaders of other traditions, and who promotes the reception (critical evaluation and discernment) of ecumenical dialogue reports that involve their church or the whole Anglican Communion.

Minister of ordination

The sending out of ministers is part of the Church's mission. A crucial aspect of episcopal ministry and mission is when the bishop presides

21. Anglican–Roman Catholic International Commission, *The Final Report* (London: CTS/SPCK, 1982), pp. 37–38 (para. 16).

22. Cf. Paul Avis, *Reshaping Ecumenical Theology* (London and New York: T&T Clark, 2010).

liturgically at ordinations. A bishop who did not ordain could hardly be a bishop. In Anglican ordinations the bishop alone ordains deacons (a practice that perhaps derives from the special relationship between the deacons and the bishop in the early Church). In the ordination of priests members of the presbyteral college lay on hands together with the bishop in solidarity with the new priest. In the ordination of bishops the archbishop normally presides and members of the episcopal college join in the laying on of hands. The ministry of ordination is an expression of episcopal oversight – the oversight of mission and ministry that is entrusted to the bishop – though as a sacramental act it is much more than that. Through episcopal ordination new ministers – bishops, priests and deacons – are incorporated within the historic ministry of the Church in continuity with the mission of the apostles, as a tangible sign that it is the same Church. In the ministry of ordination the bishop is an agent or instrument of the apostolicity of the Church, as we affirm it in the Nicene Creed, and in this sense he or she becomes a servant of the Church's essential identity. Ordination is an act of the Holy Spirit through the Church and its ministers and is intrinsic to the Church's identity.[23]

The bishop's tasks

The bishop is a key focus, instrument and agent for carrying out the three tasks that are widely recognized as central to the mission of the Church: (1) to *preach the gospel and teach the faith*; (2) to *sanctify* God's people through the sacraments; and (3) to *govern or lead* the people of God through the Church's conciliar structures and processes – its modes of consultation, discernment and decision making. Bishops preach and teach through the ministry of the word – not only in the pulpit, but in many contexts and through various media, whether formal or informal, 'in season and out of season'. They sanctify the faithful through the celebration of the sacraments, principally baptism and the Eucharist, which are always, of course, joined to the word, since the 'matter' (water, bread, wine) is given its unique meaning and significance by the 'form' (e.g. 'I baptise you'; 'Confirm, O Lord, your servant…'; 'This is my body'). They govern or lead (exercising

23. See Paul Bradshaw, 'Ordination as God's Action through the Church', pp. 8–15.

oversight) by example, teaching, consultation, discernment, building consensus and giving direction.

These three key tasks (teaching, sanctifying and governing) are outlined in the Great Commission of Matthew 28.16–20, where the risen Christ commissions his apostles to do three great things: to 'make disciples'; to baptize in the name of the Holy Trinity; and to teach his commandments. Without too much theological licence, we can see that this triple commission corresponds to the tasks of governing and leading Christ's disciples today, sanctifying God's people through the sacraments and ministering the word of God. 1 Timothy 3.1 describes the office of bishop or overseer as 'a noble task' (literally, 'a beautiful work': *kallou ergou*). A task is something laid upon one. St Augustine of Hippo comments: 'it is the name of a task, not an honour'.[24]

The three tasks are given by Christ to the whole Church, his body, so that all Christians are involved in carrying them out. But the members exercise them in different ways, according to their particular calling, whether lay person, deacon, priest or bishop. Distinct callings should be honoured. It is simply not helpful, and is actually confusing to blur these distinctions by suggesting, in the supposed interests of equally or inclusion, that, for example, lay people or deacons should preside at Holy Communion, or that oversight is shared equally between bishops and laity. But when the distinctive identity and dignity of each calling is affirmed, each one assists and strengthens the others, so that, for example, deacons assist priests and bishops and enable the laity, and bishops consult with and work alongside presbyters, deacons and laity. Christians are 'members of the household of God, built upon the foundation of the apostles and prophets, with Christ Jesus himself as the cornerstone'. As such, Christians are integrated into a beautiful structure, in which the Spirit of God dwells and through which the Spirit of God works, the Church. 'In him the whole structure is joined together and grows into a holy temple in the Lord; in whom you also are built together in the Spirit into a dwelling place for God' (Ephesians 2.19–22).

Thanks to the insights of certain early Church Fathers, followed by John Calvin and later by John Henry Newman, we are able to see that the three key tasks of teaching, sanctifying and governing

---

24. Augustine, *City of God*, trans. Henry Bettenson, ed. David Knowles (Harmondsworth: Penguin, 1972), p. 880 (Book XIX, 19).

correspond to Jesus Christ's threefold messianic (= anointed) identity as Prophet, Priest and King, an identity that he bestows upon and shares with his people who are united with him in a baptism like his own when the Holy Spirit descended upon him in anointing power (Matthew 3.16–17). The Church is a royal, prophetic priesthood (1 Peter 2.9–10). The *royal* or regal dimension corresponds to our responsibility as members of the Church with regard to its governance, each of us playing our part in caring for the life and mission of the Church. The *prophetic* dimension corresponds to teaching and proclamation – or, as 1 Peter puts it, 'proclaiming God's mighty acts' of salvation. And the *priestly* dimension equates to the work of sanctification through the sacraments, conforming us to the character and holiness of Christ. Together, these three tasks (*munera*, as the Second Vatican Council called them) comprise the mission of the Church – or to speak more correctly, the Church's part in God's mission.[25]

Three great Fathers and saints of the Church embody and represent the three tasks that make up the Church's mission: Irenaeus, Ignatius and Cyprian.[26]

> *Irenaeus*, Bishop of Lyons c. AD 185–200, is a witness to the role of the bishop as *teacher of the apostolic faith*. For Irenaeus, the bishop is the visible and personal link between each local (diocesan) church and the teaching of the Apostles. Because of his confrontation with the Gnostics, who claimed an esoteric knowledge of divine mysteries, Irenaeus attaches particular importance to the continuity of church teaching in each Christian community, teaching that is handed down through the bishop and presbyters. The seat of the bishop, his *cathedra*, symbolises the continuity of the apostolic faith. Apostolic succession is the continuity of faithful teaching of bishops within the same community, the bishop's see. Irenaeus stresses the role of the bishop as the custodian and teacher of the catholic faith.

---

25. *Christus Dominus*, §11; also *Lumen Gentium*, §21, §25. For an account of how Vatican II received these insights from the Reformation tradition, see Ormond Rush, 'The Offices of Christ, *Lumen Gentium* and the People's Sense of the Faith', *Pacifica* 16 (2003), pp. 137–152.

26. For what follows see Wright, *On Being a Bishop*, pp. 15–30.

Ignatius, Bishop of Antioch, who was martyred c. AD 107, emphasises the bishop as *president at the Church's celebration of the Eucharist*, the one who provides and oversees the sacraments and the centre of unity. Communion with the bishop underwrites the catholicity of the Church and its ministry. In Ignatius' writings we have the first clear evidence of the threefold ministry of bishop, presbyter and deacon. On his way to be martyred, Ignatius wrote to his people: 'Let all of you follow the bishop as Jesus Christ did the Father … Let no-one do any of the things that concern the church without the bishop. Let that Eucharist be considered valid which is held under the bishop, or under someone whom he appoints. Wherever the bishop appears, there let the people be, just as wherever Jesus Christ is, there is the catholic church. It is not lawful either to baptise or to hold an *agape* [love feast] without the bishop' (*To the Smyrneans*, 8). Ignatius stresses the integral place of the bishop in the Church's worship.

Cyprian, Bishop of Carthage, who was martyred in AD 258, stands for the role of *the bishop in the governance of the Church*. He witnesses to the bishop as the leader in the councils of the Church and as the bond of unity between the local churches. For Cyprian, the solidarity and collegiality of bishops is fundamental for the Church. 'The episcopate is a single whole, in which each bishop has a part.' The continuity of bishops from the Apostles, as their successors, makes them necessary for catholicity. 'The church is the people united to the bishop, the flock clinging to its shepherd. From this you should know that the bishop is in the church and the church in the bishop.' To be in communion with the catholic Church it is necessary to be in communion with and be obedient to one's bishop. Cyprian stresses the solidarity of bishops with each other and with all the faithful.

As the bishop takes his or her special part in the Church's work of teaching, sanctifying and governing, the bishop is living out the Church's messianic identity as the body of the Christ who is Prophet, Priest and King, and following in the footsteps of the great Fathers and martyrs of the early Church.

Understanding episcopacy: Some useful resources

Each member Church of the Anglican Communion has its own official texts, especially its ordination services and its canons, and perhaps various reports, setting out its understanding of episcopal ministry. Obviously it is not possible to survey them all here. But I mention below some texts best known to me. Others can be added on the companion website as suggestions come in from around the Communion in response to this book. We need to bear in mind that the older texts assume that the bishop will always be male; in some parts of the Communion the sexist pronouns are now merely historic.

Official Anglican documents on episcopal ministry and mission, including the work of the Inter-Anglican Theological and Doctrinal Commission and the Inter-Anglican Standing Commission on Ecumenical Relations, prepared for the Lambeth Conference 2008 are available at http://www.lambethconference.org/lc2008/resources/pdf/LC%20Reader.pdf

A historic benchmark text for the Anglican tradition worldwide is Thomas Cranmer's Ordinal of 1550, revised in 1662. This classic Anglican Ordinal is sometimes bound with the Book of Common Prayer (annotated edition: Brian Cummings (ed.), *The Book of Common Prayer: The Texts of 1549, 1559, and 1662* (Oxford: Oxford University Press, 2011)). While the 1662 Ordinal remains one of the three 'historic formularies' of the Church of England (the others being the Thirty-Nine Articles of Religion and the Book of Common Prayer, 1662), it is no longer in use in that Church, having been replaced by the *Common Worship Ordinal* (London: Church House Publishing, 2005; Study Edition 2007).

Another important source for understanding episcopal ministry is the Canons of the member Churches of the Anglican Communion. On this see Norman Doe, *Canon Law in the Anglican Communion* (Oxford: Clarendon Press, 1998). The summary document *The Principles of Canon Law Common to the Churches of the Anglican Communion* (London: Anglican Communion Office, 2008) has sections on church government, ministry in general and episcopacy in particular.

Other, contemporary, sources from the Church of England, which carry less (and varying) authority include:

Women Bishops in the Church of England? (The Rochester Report, London: Church House Publishing, 2004), chapter 2;
Episcopal Ministry (The Cameron Report, London: Church House Publishing, 1990);

'Apostolicity and Succession': a House of Bishops paper (London: Church House Publishing, 1991).

A concise introduction is provided in C. J. Podmore, 'The Church of England's Understanding of Episcopacy', *Theology*, May–June 2006.

Resources from The Episcopal Church (including extracts from Church of England documents) are provided in J. Robert Wright (ed.), *On Being a Bishop: Papers on Episcopacy from the Moscow Consultation 1992* (New York: The Church Hymnal Corporation, 1993).

An Anglican theology of ministry, including the episcopate, is given in Paul Avis, *A Ministry Shaped by Mission* (London and New York: T&T Clark, 2005). And an apologia for the significance of episcopacy for Christian unity is offered in Paul Avis, *Reshaping Ecumenical Theology* (London and New York: T&T Clark, 2010), chapter 7: 'Episcopacy: Focus of Unity or Cause of Division?'

A great Anglican work on the gospel, the Church and the ministry of bishops is A. M. Ramsey, *The Gospel and the Catholic Church* (London: Longmans, Green & Co., 1936; reissued several times).

Michael Ramsey's *The Christian Priest Today* (London: SPCK, 1972; revised edition 1985) also has a chapter on 'The Bishop'.

A seminal work on the role of the bishop within an overall understanding of the Church, from the Greek Orthodox tradition, but congenial to the Anglican tradition, is John Zizioulas, *Eucharist, Bishop, Church: The Unity of the Church in the Divine Eucharist and the Bishop during the First Three Centuries* (2nd edition, trans. E. Theokritoff, Brookline, MA: Holy Cross Orthodox Press, 2001).

The Second Vatican Council issued a *Decree on the Pastoral Office of the Bishops in the Church (Christus Dominus)*, which can be found in: W. M. Abbott, S.J. (ed.), *The Documents of Vatican II* (London and Dublin: Geoffrey Chapman, 1966), pp. 396–429; Austin Flannery, O. P. (ed.), *Vatican Council II, Volume I, The Conciliar and Post Conciliar Documents* ('new revised edition', New York: Costello; Dublin: Dominican Publications, 1992), pp. 564–590; or online at http://www.ewtn.com/library/councils/v2bishop.htm

Pope John Paul II issued an Apostolic Exhortation *Pastores Gregis*, on the ministry of bishops, following the Synod of Bishops in Rome in 1990: http://www.vatican.va/holy_father/john_paul_ii/apost_exhortations/documents/hf_jp-ii_exh_20031016_pastores-gregis_en.html

The most widely received multilateral ecumenical text that deals with
episcopacy is *Baptism, Eucharist and Ministry* (Geneva: World
Council of Churches, 1982), in which the Lambeth Conference
of 1988 was able to discern 'the faith of the Church through
the ages': http://www.oikoumene.org/en/resources/documents/
commissions/faith-and-order/i-unity-the-church-and-its-mission/
baptism-eucharist-and-ministry-faith-and-order-paper-no-111
-the-lima-text

A key ecumenical text for Anglicans is the early report of the Anglican
Roman-Catholic International Commission (ARCIC), 'Ministry
and Ordination' (*The Final Report*, London: CTS/SPCK, 1982):
http://www.prounione.urbe.it/dia-int/arcic/doc/e_arcic_final
.html. Also, though with some ambiguities, *The Gift of Authority:
Authority in the Church III* (Toronto: Anglican Book Centre;
London: Catholic Truth Society; New York: Church Publishing Inc.,
1999): http://www.prounione.urbe.it/dia-int/arcic/doc/e
_arcicII_05.html

The Cyprus Agreed Statement of the International Commission
for Anglican-Orthodox Theological Dialogue *The Church of the
Triune God* (London: Anglican Communion Office, 2006) contains
valuable material on episcopacy in Section V.

Other important texts, especially for the British and Irish Anglican
Churches, are *Together in Mission and Ministry: The Porvoo
Common Statement, etc.* (London: Church House Publishing, 1992)
and *Called to Witness and Service: The Reuilly Common Statement
with Essays on Church, Eucharist and Ministry* (London: Church
House Publishing, 1999).

Various reports of the International Anglican Liturgical
Consultation (now Commission) touch helpfully on the ministry
of bishops: David R. Holeton (ed.), *Renewing the Anglican
Eucharist* (Cambridge: Grove Books, 1996); David R. Holeton
(ed.), *Anglican Orders and Ordinations* (Cambridge: Grove
Books, 1997); Paul Gibson (ed.), *Anglican Ordination Rites: The
Berkeley Statement: 'To Equip the Saints'* (Cambridge: Grove
Books, 2002).

Archbishop Rowan Williams contributed a small gem on this subject
to a symposium on primacy (the role of archbishops and presiding
bishops) at St Vladimir's Seminary, New York, in 2008: http://
rowanwilliams.archbishopofcanterbury.org/articles.php/1357/
rome-constantinople-and-canterbury-mother-churches

Bishops who heard Archbishop Rowan Williams' retreat addresses
and Presidential Addresses at the 2008 Lambeth Conference
will need no encouragement to revisit them. And bishops who
were not present, for various reasons, will find much to stimulate
reflection on the ministry of a bishop: http://rowanwilliams
.archbishopofcanterbury.org/tags.php?action=view&id=63, etc.
An early paper by Rowan Williams is worth digging out: 'Authority
and the Bishop in the Church', in Mark Santer (ed.), *Their Lord
and Ours: Approaches to Authority, Community and the Unity of
the Church*; Foreword by the Archbishop of Canterbury [Robert
Runcie] (London: SPCK, 1982), pp. 90–112.

Chapter 3

THE BISHOP'S AUTHORITY

Authority plays a key role in the Christian churches. There is probably no single part of church life where authority is not an issue – and authority is always controversial. Reading the church press you could think that Christians are obsessed with authority – and we probably are. Questions of authority are also at the heart of ecclesiology, theological reflection on the nature and mission of the Church. So there is a need in all churches to develop a serviceable theology of authority and a salutary practice of authority. The history of the Christian Church could be summed up in the phrase 'In search of authority' – that is to say, cogent, persuasive and salutary forms of authority in the Church.[1] It is arguable that a large part of what is distinctive of Anglicanism is its characteristic approach to issues of authority. We could even say that Anglicanism is called to pioneer a particular kind of salutary authority. What that might be will, I hope, become clear as we proceed.

The theological discussion of authority falls into three main areas. (a) The *sources* of authority: Scripture, tradition, reason, conscience; what experience teaches us; the role of non-theological knowledge and insight. To put it another way: where do we look for guidance and inspiration, for norms and parameters, for models and precedents when facing new questions and challenges in our faith and in church teaching? (b) The *structures* of authority and how they function in the institutional life of the Church. In other words, the personal, collegial and communal forms of oversight, as the Faith and Order report *Baptism, Eucharist and Ministry* puts it.[2] This aspect of authority

1. I have applied this idea of the search for sound and salutary forms of authority to the formative centuries of the Anglican tradition in Paul Avis, *In Search of Authority: Anglican Theological Method from the Reformation to the Enlightenment* (London and New York: Bloomsbury, T&T Clark, 2014).
2. *Baptism, Eucharist and Ministry* (Geneva: World Council of Churches, 1982), M 26.

refers to the conciliar life of the Church – its forms of discernment, consultation, debate, dialogue, decision making and the reception of those decisions.[3] (c) The *dynamics* of authority: how authority works, how it is received and experienced, how it plays out in relation to issues of leadership, example, vision, strategy, obedience, consent and conflict. It is the second and third of these, the structures of authority and governance and where episcopal ministry fits into these, and the dynamics of authority and leadership, as these affect the bishop's ministry, that I will discuss here.

Defining authority

It is not unusual to hear bishops lamenting their 'lack of authority' or complaining, 'I don't actually have much [or "any"] power.' A bishop often feels frustrated and sometimes powerless, seeing what he or she thinks needs to be done, but feeling helpless to implement it; or perhaps seeing one of their clergy going wrong and being unable to prevent it. But in fact bishops always have both power and authority, properly understood. It is vital to grasp the connection between authority and power, and also the distinction between them. So what is the difference between the two and how does it show itself in the bishop's ministry?[4]

Power can be defined as the ability to make people do what we want them to do, believe what we want them to believe and want what we want them to want. In other words, power is the capacity to obtain compliance with our wishes and desires, even when that compliance is given reluctantly and unwillingly. Power takes many shapes, ranging from brute force at one extreme to subtle emotional manipulation at the other. It takes economic, military, political, social and religious forms, to name but a few. Power is a morally neutral commodity: it can be put to good or bad uses. What power alone does not and cannot do is to evoke the free and willing consent of those to whom it is directed. It cannot induce voluntary cooperation, freely given – and that, of course,

---

3. See Paul Avis, *Beyond the Reformation? Authority, Primacy and Unity in the Conciliar Tradition* (London and New York: T&T Clark, 2006).

4. See Paul Avis, *Authority, Leadership and Conflict in the Church* (London: Mowbray, 1992); S. W. Sykes, *Power and Christian Theology* (London and New York: Continuum, 2006); Martyn Percy, *Power and the Church* (London: Cassell, 1998).

is the essential condition for getting anything done in the Church. As Milton puts it, in the mouths of the angels: ' ... freely we serve, Because we freely love'.[5] But to wield power has been generally recognized as morally bad for us; it carries a health warning. As Lord Acton, the Roman Catholic historian of the latter part of the nineteenth century, famously puts it: 'Power tends to corrupt, and absolute power corrupts absolutely'.[6] Power is a dangerous commodity; it consorts uneasily with grace and the gospel and our call to serve – but it is unavoidable.

The exercise of power is inescapable. Power relations are synonymous with social relations. There is no relationship that does not involve power, usually asymmetrically, in an unequal way. Power play is all-pervasive, but power is distributed unevenly. The 'powerless' are the oppressed, the marginalized, the victims. Powerlessness is also bad for our souls and antithetical to well-being. Powerlessness is not an exegesis of the gospel, as is sometimes suggested, and is not equivalent to Christlikeness. Without any power, we are less than fully human. Powerlessness is an affront to human dignity and is destructive of a proper sense of self-worth. Those who exercise leadership, in the Church or in any other institution, are necessarily exercising power in and over their constituency. But it is worth noting that those who freely respond to leadership, without being coerced, also have a certain power – the power to give or to withhold their consent and support. Bishops will be acutely sensitive to this factor – the need to win the freely given cooperation of the faithful in fulfilling the tasks of the Church.

The modern Christian Church is in effect a voluntary organization. It is very largely made up of volunteers (the laity) who give their time, energy and financial support freely because that is what they want to do and what they believe to be right. But the clergy also give of themselves sacrificially because they are doing it 'as unto the Lord'. So mere assertion of power by those in authority – supposing *per impossibile* that it were possible – the giving of orders and commands, would have little purchase on their motives. Since the Church is a community of those who voluntarily adhere to it, people can always vote with their feet. In reality Church leaders have little or no power to enforce the compliance of lay people, not even in hierarchical churches that threaten and impose spiritual sanctions, such as exclusion from communion, as the Roman

5. John Milton, *Paradise Lost*, V, 538–9: *The English Poems of John Milton*, ed. H. C. Beeching (London: Oxford University Press, 1913), p. 220.

6. Lord Acton letter to Mandell Creighton, 5 April 1887, in Roland Hill, *Lord Acton* (New Haven and London: Yale University Press, 2000), p. 300.

Catholic Church does for the divorced and remarried. The vast majority of church leaders are not under the illusion that they have that kind of power and they do not seek it. The key to motivating lay people and clergy to pull together in a common cause lies not in power but in authority.

Authority, in contrast to power, can be defined as the ability to win people voluntarily to your way of thinking and to the kind of actions that you want to see. In other words, authority is the capacity to obtain freely motivated consent or support and is a key component of leadership. Authority is related to power, and in one sense is one of its many-faceted forms. We could say that authority is legitimated power, power that has the right to seek freely given compliance. The Greek Gospels generally distinguish between *dunamis* (power) and *exousia* (authority), though these terms are not always clearly distinguished. When the woman with the haemorrhage touched the hem of his garment Jesus became aware that *dunamis* had gone out of him (Mark 5.30). He performed 'deeds of power' (*dunamis*: Matthew 11. 21, 23). But what legitimated that power was his God-given authority. Jesus had 'authority (*exousia*) on earth to forgive sins' (Mark 2.10). At the Ascension the risen Christ gave the Great Commission: 'All *exousia* in heaven and on earth has been given to me; go, therefore ...' (Matthew 28.16–20).

So those who have authority have a recognized right to lead, guide, teach and show the way (and this takes us to the heart of the bishop's ministry). That right is freely accorded to them by those who recognize that they have certain attributes that qualify them to exercise that particular authority. They have that authority because it is recognized by others. Authority, for a Christian, is always a modulated, self-doubting, broken-backed form of power. It has most integrity when it is always somewhat afraid of itself. But at the end of the day, authority needs to have the courage of its convictions.

If power needs very careful handling, so does authority: it is not a tame alternative. The modern world, with all its complexities and dilemmas, is characterized by a profound ambivalence towards authority. On the one hand, there is strong distrust of established authority. There is a widespread suspicion of authoritative institutions such as governments, made up of politicians, which attempt to tell people what they can and cannot do, and churches, which not only tell people what they can and cannot do, but also what they should and should not believe. It was this sense of authority that Hannah Arendt had in mind, I believe, when she wrote words that should give churches and bishops pause for thought: 'Authority has vanished from the modern world.' Arendt added, 'We are no longer in a position to know what authority really is.'[7] Arendt was right to the extent that there is no longer, in the developed world, any human authority that is simply taken on trust, unquestioningly. In every case, even when eventually, as with state laws, we have to comply, we ask, 'Are they right? Can I accept this? Does this square with what my reason and conscience, my sense of personal integrity, tell me?' A recent study of Roman Catholics in Britain revealed that, in taking personal decisions, the number of professing Roman Catholics who looked to their church leaders (priests or bishops) for guidance was 0 per cent (that is not a misprint), though 8 per cent took seriously the tradition and teaching of the Church.[8]

The other side of this ambivalence with regard to authority is that modern culture often manifests a thirst for authority, a need for answers, someone to entrust or surrender oneself to. This longing can easily degenerate into a passion to abandon oneself blindly to a leader in uncritical discipleship and devotion. It may seem that Anglicanism, with its tradition (in part) of sobriety and moderation, is inimical to this particular pathology, but creating unhealthy dependence between leader and led is an ever-present danger in all traditions. Bishops have their devotees and their despisers; they cannot have the former without the latter and they would be better without both and the Church would be a happier place altogether. To the world at large, to those Christians who never meet them in the flesh, bishops (and even more, archbishops) are hardly real people: they are projections, figments, symbols, ciphers. Even more so than the parochial clergy, bishops are ambiguous love–hate figures; people tend to feel ambivalently about them. They can be appropriated for various ulterior purposes, one of the most significant and unhealthy of these being emotional dependence.

Bishops, like all leaders, extend emotional support to individuals among their following. In doing so they affirm the value of those individuals to the organization, in this case the Church (and that inevitably includes their support for the leader), and so strengthen motivation to conform and to serve among those whom the Church needs to carry out its work. Good leaders build self-confidence in those who follow; they set people on their own feet and help them to get

7. Hannah Arendt (ed), 'What Is Authority?', *Between Past and Future* (Harmondsworth: Penguin, 1977), pp. 9–10.

8. Linda Woodhead, 'Endangered Species', *The Tablet*, 16 November 2013, pp. 6–7; http://faithdebates.org.uk/blog/surveys-reveal-widening-gulf-catholics -church-teaching/

on with their tasks and their lives, enabling them to move on without the need to keep coming back for reassurance and approval. The very best leaders aim to make themselves dispensable; the ship can sail on without them. The litmus test for bishops, as for priests, is whether the bishop is aware that she/he needs the people more than the people need him or her. So leaders will be sensitive to the dependency issues that are endemic in their situation and will gently but firmly give dependence back. How to affirm and give support and guidance without creating and fostering unhealthy dependence, and so slipping into blatant power play, is a skill that belongs to true leadership and qualifies it as therapeutic leadership, one that fosters wholeness and integrity in all persons who experience it on the receiving end.

So what characterizes authority is a recognized right to lead, direct or instruct. How is that recognized right acquired? It is not acquired automatically, painlessly or immediately, and cannot be conferred by higher authority in such an automatic or immediate way, but has to be accorded, earned or won, as when we speak of someone 'earning our respect'. Authority can be earned, accorded or awarded in several complementary ways:

(a) One way in which authority can accrue to a person is through appointment or election to an *office* (such as bishop, archbishop, or even pope), an office that has some public standing and recognition. The office is in existence prior to any individual incumbent and will continue after they have gone. It takes its significance from the traditions and structures of the institution to which it belongs as that institution endures through time. Bishops are immersed in the institution because it is what gives them the office that makes them bishops. Therefore, bishops cannot sit lightly to the institution – and certainly they cannot publicly run it down – without cutting off the branch on which they are sitting. To the extent that the Church as an institution is respected, the office holder will be respected, at least initially. But the office does not confer moral validation on the office-holder. It works in reverse too: bishops who are respected because of the quality of their ministry cause the Church to be taken seriously, to be listened to with attention and respect. But on its own this mode of awarding authority, that is to say through office, cuts little ice today. As Lord Acton insisted, 'There is no worse heresy than that the office sanctifies the holder of it.'[9] The authority of expertise, experience, example and manifest personal integrity is much more persuasive in western culture. However, office remains important for the Church, because it underlines the fact that, in Christian terms, no one can take authority to themselves: it has to be given and received before it can function and it can only function within a given framework in which many others have an investment and a stake.

(b) A second way in which authority is conferred is through *expertise*, that is to say through mastery of a specialized area of useful knowledge or possession of skills that are widely valued. The status given to eminent scientists in modern culture is a prime example of the authority of expertise. (The media play into this excessive deference to science by dubbing them all generically 'scientists', rather than physicists, chemists, biologists, pharmacologists, astronomers, geologists, zoologists, epidemiologists, etc.) Scientists are held in awe because they are believed to understand mysteries that are lost on ordinary people and to have the skills and technology to arrive at further exciting and life-enhancing discoveries. Through their knowledge, it is believed, they can make human life better, happier and longer. Clergy, including bishops, also have expert knowledge of mysteries that are believed to be vital for human well-being, even if not everyone subscribes to that belief. Their expertise includes knowledge of the Scriptures and theology, together with pastoral and liturgical skills, hence the importance of scholarly habits and wisdom in the bishop's profile. But on its own this knowledge could remain at a purely academic or theoretical level and not be effectively deployed, so it cannot stand alone.

(c) A third way in which authority is credibly awarded is through the force of *example*, that is to say through outstanding personal qualities and the wisdom gained in the tough school of experience. Leaders do not need to cultivate a charismatic persona in order to have authority. Charismatic figures have authority, first through exceptional personal endowment of a magnetic quality and, second, through the way that it is cultivated and displayed. They embody certain values that people long for. Their life reveals what people desire for themselves. Through personal magnetism they are able to attract followers, for good or ill. The cult of celebrity and of charisma in western civilization is a distortion of the proper authority of example, because celebrities are constructs of the

9. Acton letter to Mandell Creighton, 5 April 1887, in Hill, *Lord Acton*, p. 300.

media: no one knows what 'celebrities' are really like as individuals. They are fictive symbols or ciphers, rather than examples. But in a Christian context the relevant personal qualities to which authority accrues are holiness, prayerfulness, humility, dedication, self-sacrifice, compassion, etc., and these are not particularly charismatic, that is to say expressive qualities, qualities that can be displayed to public advantage. They cannot be put on for show, but emerge only from spiritual integrity. Authenticity is a condition of authority and always precedes it. Nothing is more lethal to authority than a whiff of hypocrisy or posturing or playing to the gallery, such as saying or doing things to try to make people like you.

Where the three *foci* of office, expertise and example come together (as they need to do in the case of every bishop, in the Church of God), and are used with divine wisdom and prudence, it results in a very strong combination that makes for effective Christian leadership.

Authority and conflict

Rowan Williams once made the cryptic but seminal comment that the bishop's authority is the authority to unify.[10] That comment is likely to produce a frustrated outburst from bishops to the effect that that is all very well, but they are dealing all the time, not with some serene experience of unity – as though the bishop were, by his or her very existence, the still centre of a turbulent world – but with issues of conflict, rather than unity: disaffection on the part of individual clergy or laity, failure of clergy to live up to the expected standard, personality clashes within the clergy team or between clergy and parish officers, and square pegs in round holes – not to mention issues concerned with diminishing resources, a defensive, inward-looking attitude and lack of evangelistic zeal. Quite a package of issues! Thus a bishop may protest, 'Most of the time I am not unifying – that would be a luxury – I am reconciling, mediating, disciplining, repairing relationships, exhorting, counselling. I'm engaged in damage limitation, "ambulance work". I don't see myself as a focus and

10. Rowan Williams, 'Authority and the Bishop in the Church', in Mark Santer (ed.), *Their Lord and Ours: Approaches to Authority, Community and the Unity of the Church*; Foreword by the Archbishop of Canterbury [Robert Runcie] (London: SPCK, 1982), pp. 90–112 at p. 99.

sign of unity; unity seems altogether too elevated, too serene a word for church life on the ground.' In fact, in that sort of scenario, the bishop is exercising the authority to unify – to heal, repair, restore. It may not be very glamorous work, but it is the proper unifying work of a bishop. Rowan Williams expressly says that the authority to unify is not about avoiding conflict.[11] So how are unity and conflict related?

There is no unity without conflict. Unity and conflict are inter-related and interdependent. Authority always engenders conflict. Even when it appears to succeed in repressing or restraining conflict by coercion, the absence of overt conflict is merely temporary: the pressure is building up under the surface and will eventually erupt. What we need to aim for is a way of holding conflict within unity, minimizing the destructive effects of unrestrained conflict and instead harnessing the energy of conflict to serve the ends of the Church.[12] Alasdair MacIntyre has reminded us that, in a healthy society or community, conflict is perennial because there will always be argument about the aims or goals of that society. The tradition that helps to give the community its identity is constituted by ongoing debate – argument – about the nature of the 'goods', the pursuit of which gives the community its *raison d'être*. As MacIntyre puts it: 'Traditions, when vital, embody continuities of conflict … A living tradition, then, is an historically extended, socially embodied argument, and argument precisely in part about the goods which constitute that tradition.'[13] This seems an apt description of the history of the Christian Church: the Church knows all about passionate debate, conscientious dissent and violent argument.

'Conflict is endemic in human affairs', wrote Geoffrey Vickers, 'and its management is the most characteristically human function and skill'.[14] If conflict is unavoidable, the leader's aim must be to harness it for the good of the organization or institution, to channel its energies into constructive debate and activity that promotes the aims of the organization. It falls to leaders to try to negotiate a *modus vivendi*

---

11. Williams, 'Authority and the Bishop in the Church', pp. 90–112.

12. In this section I draw on chapter 10 of Avis, *Authority, Leadership and Conflict in the Church*.

13. Alasdair MacIntyre, *After Virtue: A Study in Moral Theory* (2nd edition, London: Duckworth; Notre Dame, IN: University of Notre Dame Press, 1985), p. 222.

14. Geoffrey Vickers, *Making Institutions Work* (London: Associated Business Programmes, 1973), p. 153.

between the contentions of rival groups and interests, on the one hand, and the overall aims of the organization, the common good, on the other – which Selznick describes as 'bind[ing] parochial group egotism to larger loyalties and aspirations'.[15]

The role of the leader in conflict is not the same as the role of the manager. The manager's task is to try to contain conflict, to mediate and to reconcile. But the leader's calling is to seek to harness conflict to serve the mission of the institution. The secret here is to divert conflicting energies away from organizational infighting to confront challenges that emanate from outside, from the cultural, ideological environment. Groups should be encouraged, indeed urged, to devote their energies to what they do best, whether it is personal evangelism (evangelicals), awesome worship (Catholics) or dialogue and social concern (liberals). Since all three activities belong to the core tasks of the Church, competing groups can serve the common cause by doing what they are happiest doing. The leader – in this case the bishop – affirms the value of all three spheres of action to the overall mission of the Church by both word and deed, leading by example in personal excellence of evangelization, worship and thoughtful conversation and theological reflection, combined with social concern and initiatives.

The deleterious effects of unrestrained conflict – conflict that gets out of hand – are obvious. It reduces collaboration within the organization; it leaves individuals battered, discouraged and unproductive. It wastefully diverts energy from productive effort to internecine warfare. It sets up a structural polarization of contending parties that can paralyse the organization. On the one hand, conflict that is managed or worked with can be a source of vitality for an organization. It gives space for internal interest groups to pursue their aims, some of which may turn out to be for the overall benefit of the organization. Conflict that is worked with constructively may also open up the system (if we think of organizations such as the Church on the model of a system) to its environment as fresh energies are drawn in, and with them fresh insights. Managed conflict can serve to clarify the best interests of the organization, correct imbalances of power and stimulate reform and renewal.[16] Irenic bishops should note Charles Handy's warning that

15. Philip Selznick, *Leadership in Administration: A Sociological Interpretation* (New York: Harper, 1957), p. 93.

16. Selznick, *Leadership in Administration: A Sociological Interpretation*, pp. 94, 368.

all attempts to bring about a 'totally homogeneous, unargumentative, non-disputatious' state of affairs in organizations have resulted in poor productivity and low morale.[17]

Slightly against the general tenor of this handbook, which has concentrated on theological principles, I am now going to become quite down to earth and to offer some practical guidelines to assist the bishop in the delicate task of harnessing conflict. But I hope that these guidelines can be seen as simply concrete embodiments of the principles that we have been studying.[18]

1. 'Don't be afraid.' The first and most basic point that I want to make to bishops about handling conflict is simply this: 'Don't be afraid of conflict.' Some bishops' approach to situations of conflict is purely cosmetic, that is to say superficial and concerned with window-dressing. They try by all means to smooth things over, to speak and act as though there was not in fact a serious issue to be dealt with. But often in situations of tension and conflict there is a real difference of perception, a rival cognitive perspective that arises from an alternative social, cultural and theological hinterland. What is needed in such a situation is a profound hermeneutical understanding of the other, skilled interpretation founded on the humility to listen without hurrying to the seat of judgement. And this deep empathetic engagement is only possible if we are genuinely not afraid of conflict. When we are afraid of anything, the hormone adrenaline kicks in, driving the two instinctive responses of 'fight' and 'flight'. Both of these reactions are fatal to the possibility of bringing healing to situations of conflict. 'Fight' means that we respond to conflict aggressively, weighing in on one side or the other. But this the bishop, who is the shepherd of the souls of all of his or her people, cannot do. To become a protagonist in a situation of conflict that is internal to a parish or congregation is a tactic that the bishop cannot afford to indulge. But 'flight' is equally useless, because it represents an escape from threatening forces of conflict that are bound to make anyone feel vulnerable, but need to be tackled. The advice, 'Fear not conflict', is counter-

---

17. Charles Handy, *Understanding Organisations* (3rd edition, Harmondsworth: Penguin, 1985), p. 255.

18. Similar points are developed in Avis, *Authority, Leadership and Conflict in the Church*, pp. 121–32.

intuitive; it is natural to fear it. The path to effective mediation and perhaps eventual reconciliation is one that involves accepting our own vulnerability in the face of hostile attitudes, towards either ourselves or others, and courageously addressing the conflicted situation in the strength that comes from above, so that we may become trusted figures, whose humanity and integrity are respected on all sides. That is the only feasible position from which to take steps to harness the energies generated by conflict.

2. Listen more than you speak. Bishops are always speaking. Often they are called upon to do so. Sometimes they seem to think that they have failed if they have not said the last word in any discussion with their clergy or laity. But we learn more by listening than by speaking – except for learning from our own mistakes! The old proverb says, 'Speech is silver; silence is golden.' Listen – reflect prayerfully – speak: that is the best order of events for a bishop. And when the times comes for spoken intervention, always be constructive, so that even the kind of difficult decisions about budgets, staffing, deployment and so on, that have to be tackled from time to time, can be set within a wider positive framework and vision, for this brings hope and hope spurs people to act.

3. In your private devotions pray by name for all those with whom you have personal dealings, especially those you find difficult. Intercede for their well-being and blessing at the hand of God. To their own master – rather than to you – they ultimately stand or fall. By the same token, it is wise as well as just to offer hospitality to all, not merely to those whom we find agreeable company or are known to be sympathetic to our vision. 'Thereby some have entertained angels unawares' (Hebrews 13.1, KJB). If your hospitality is declined by partisan persons, you have lost nothing, but those who have refused it are thereby morally diminished.

4. Give away any praise and prestige that comes your way. We all need praise when it is our due and none of us is averse to a modicum of prestige in one corner of our lives or another. But when we gather praise and prestige to ourselves we inflate our personality and increase the distance of ourselves from others whom we seek to serve. I find it an unattractive practice in some churches when someone is deputed to warm up the congregation's receptiveness to the sermon by lauding the preacher in inordinate terms, as God's gift to the Church. John the Baptist got it right when he said, 'I am a voice' (John 1.23). When we give away and pass on praise and

prestige we affirm others and lessen the distance between them and ourselves, so that we may learn and receive from them and they from us.

5. Work collaboratively with your team and thereby promote ownership of the work. A sense of ownership boosts motivation and motivation in turn generates energy. The programmes that the bishop wants to see implemented belong not to the bishop, but to the church as a body. They should not be labelled (or even thought of by anyone) as 'the bishop's initiative' or 'the bishop's vision', even if the bishop has been the main catalyst to bring them about. It is as though the bishop's driving force has to be set aside so that others can share in ownership of the projects. Once agreed, the ideas become the property of the church and all its members are called to work together in the common enterprise. A collectively worked out and agreed strategy binds people together in a common purpose.

6. Respect local loyalties and ancient boundaries. Eventually these may need to be challenged if they genuinely hamper effective mission, but the challenge is unlikely to be successful unless the bishop has first both understood and shown respect for what people locally hold dear. We are talking about landmarks of the mind as well as landmarks of geography, contours of the collective local psyche as well as the landscape of the parish. Ancient boundaries and local loyalties are embedded in the collective identity of the community. This is a principle to be borne in mind particularly when it comes to making changes: questions of pastoral reorganization, grouping parishes together, amalgamating congregations and redefining parish boundaries and diocesan structures. The old proverb says, 'It's a bad workman who blames his tools.' Equally, a poor leader tends to blame the structures when things do not go as well as was hoped. The leader who is both humble and imaginative does not feel the need to make his or her mark on the structures and will be able largely to work through them for the time being.

7. Reward excellence combined with commitment. Because the modern churches are voluntary organizations, their members give their time, talents and energies freely, provided that they are motivated to do so. Bishops today are not in a position to give material rewards. Even the sort of senior positions in the diocese that fall within the bishop's patronage are a mixed blessing – sometimes a poisoned chalice – invariably bringing increased workload and enhanced stress levels. But generous quantities of

appreciation can go a long way to making colleagues feel valued. Even such apparently small gestures, such as renaming the 'Bishop's Staff Meeting' the 'Bishop's Team meeting' can enhance colleagues' sense of involvement and willingness to share responsibility. However, in affirming the value of individuals to the common enterprise, the bishop needs to take care not to raise unrealistic expectations with individuals about future prospects, expectations that the bishop may in the end not be able to fulfil. Finally, it is not simply talent, outstanding ability, that deserves recognition, but talent combined with commitment, that is to say 'hard graft' on behalf of the organization – in this case the diocese or the wider church. While everyone who makes a contribution to the common task deserves appreciation, the mission of the Church needs persons with exceptional gifts – they are God's gifts after all (1 Corinthians 12.4–11; Ephesians 4.7–11). One of the bishop's roles is to value and cherish all persons for whom she/he has pastoral responsibility and to provide, as far as she/he can, opportunities for those gifts to be further developed. In this way the bishop becomes an instrument of the Holy Spirit, a midwife to bring to birth effective mission and ministry in Christ's Church.

8. Stick to your calling, to what was laid upon you at your ordination and do not let the pressing needs of institutional nitty-gritty deflect you from it. Above all, the bishop's calling is this: to expound the Scriptures and teach the faith and to provide for this to happen in every parish of the diocese; to preside at the sacraments and to provide sacramental ministry throughout the diocese; to offer pastoral care, guidance, support and oversight of the flock and to ensure that this is available throughout the diocese. The bishop is not called to become enmeshed in organizational wrangling, horse-trading, negotiating or even mediating (except perhaps with and between his/her closest colleagues, who in practice have no one they can look to for this role except the bishop). In a sense, the bishop is to be above the fray. Stanley Hauerwas puts my point in his usual trenchant manner: 'Bishops have no authority [these days] because they now understand their office primarily in terms of being a CEO of a dysfunctional company.'[19] But that

---

19. Stanley Hauerwas, *Approaching the End: Eschatological Reflections on Church, Politics and Life* (Grand Rapids: Eerdmans; London: SCM Press, 2014), p. 89.

is the exact antithesis of how episcopal ministry is understood in this book. The Church's tasks (*munera*) are the bishop's tasks; they embody the Great Commission of Matthew 20.16–end: 'make disciples ... baptise ... teach'.

The bishop's role as the Church seeks to discern God's will

Hearing the word

The churches of the Anglican Communion, like all Christian churches, constantly seek the will of God for their life and mission.[20] So important is this aspect of the Church's life that the Church could be defined as the community that waits upon God, listens for the guidance of the Holy Spirit and hears the voice of the Good Shepherd. To do this is absolutely basic to being the Church. Martin Luther wrote in 1537, 'Thank God, a seven-year-old child knows what the Church is, namely holy believers and sheep who hear the voice of their shepherd.'[21] We hear God's word above all in Jesus Christ, the word incarnate. Christians may be described in the words of the title of one of Karl Rahner's major works as *Hearers of the Word*.[22] As we hear, we understand, and as we understand we discern what the Lord is teaching us, and as we discern what the Lord is teaching us we move towards obedience to God's word. This applies both to our individual Christian discipleship and to the Church corporately. It is said that, 'Generally speaking, bishops are generally speaking.' As those called to speak, bishops must be first of all those who listen, who hear, who understand and exercise discernment.

The need to be attuned to the word of God suggests that Anglican churches need both a theology and a practice of hearing, discernment

20. This section draws some material from Paul Avis, 'Conciliarity in the Anglican Communion: History, Theology and Polemic', in *Cristianesimo nella storia*, 32.3 (2011), pp. 1085–1104. For detailed substantiation of my argument I refer to Avis, *Beyond the Reformation? Authority, Primacy and Unity in the Conciliar Tradition*.

21. Smalcald Articles XII, *The Book of Concord*, ed. T. G. Tappert (Philadelphia: Fortress Press, 1959), p. 315.

22. K. Rahner, *Hearers of the Word: Laying the Foundation for a Philosophy of Religion*, rev. ed., trans. Michael Richards (New York: Herder and Herder, 1969).

and decision making. In fact we have these already. The Anglican theology of discernment is to be found in the writings of Anglican theologians on authority, from the Reformers to the present time. Within this corpus of Anglican theology we may distinguish the three strands that we have noted already above, relating to the *sources*, the *structures* and the *dynamics* of authority. The first focuses on the respective roles of (principally) Scripture, tradition and reason as sources of guidance for the Church. Among these Scripture is supreme. The Preface to the Church of England's Declaration of Assent (Canon C 15) speaks of 'the faith uniquely revealed in the holy Scriptures'. Scripture is not regarded as given in order to provide binding rules for the outward ordering of the Church, its polity and worship, as certain Protestants and Puritans mistakenly held, but rather to show the way of salvation – in whom we should put our trust and how we should live as disciples of Christ – the most important things of all.[23] Scripture, interpreted in the light of tradition and by using all the sources of knowledge and insight that we can bring to bear ('reason'), taking our conscience as our guide, is where we find God's word to us. But how does that process of interpretation happen *corporately*, in the life of the Church as a whole?

Conciliarity

The way that we hear the word of God, discern the will of God and take decisions in the Church falls within the dimension of conciliarity. What do we mean by conciliarity? Conciliarity is the means of ordering the life of the Church as a coherent whole in a way that involves the whole Church representatively. What drives the conciliar dimension of the Church is a longing for unity and coherence, and that means consensus, being of one mind. So the quest for consensus in the Church is a vital aspect of conciliarity. The Church in this context is not understood as a collection of local congregations or dioceses that may happen to come together from time to time for their mutual advantage. Rather the Church is understood in a strongly realist or sacramental sense as the Body of Christ. Conciliarity stands for the principle of the whole body of the Church taking responsibility for its mission, where mission in its broadest sense, its totality, embraces doctrine, worship, ministry, discipleship and evangelization. Conciliarity invokes the authority that

---

23. See further, Avis, *In Search of Authority: Anglican Theological Method from the Reformation to the Enlightenment*.

is distributed throughout the whole body; it gathers and focuses that authority when the Church comes together, in a representative way, to take counsel for its well-being and the advancement of its mission.

The concept of conciliarity provides the theological framework in which all baptized Christians, gathered into communities by the ministry of word and sacrament under the oversight of their pastors, discharge their share of responsibility for the life of the Church according to their various callings. Conciliarity equates to what the World Council of Churches' Faith and Order document of 1982, *Baptism, Eucharist and Ministry*, called the 'communal' dimension of ministry.[24] Within this communal dimension the other two dimensions that are identified by *Baptism, Eucharist and Ministry*, the collegial and the personal, find their place. So conciliarity provides the broadest context within which other expressions of oversight are located, like concentric ripples on a pond. The *collegiality* of bishops, with their special responsibility for doctrine, worship and ministry, with each other and with the presbyters who share oversight locally with their bishops, is exercised within the broader reality of conciliarity. The *personal* dimension of ministry and oversight (e.g. the larger responsibilities of archbishops) functions first within the sphere of collegiality and then within the sphere of conciliarity. As a report of the 1968 Lambeth Conference puts it: 'the collegiality of the episcopate must always be seen in the context of the conciliar character of the Church, involving the *consensus fidelium* [consensus of the faithful], in which the episcopate has its place.'[25]

Three constitutional principles

Three constitutional principles emerged in the conciliar thought of the pre-Reformation period. They can be seen as explications of the old adage: 'What affects all must be approved by all.' This dictum goes back to antiquity and was incorporated in medieval canon law. It was invoked by the great pre-Reformation conciliarists and was still a live issue at the time of the Reformation, being quoted by Martin Luther on occasion. It is regarded as an unquestionable axiom of the conciliar tradition.

24. *Baptism, Eucharist and Ministry*, M 26.
25. *The Lambeth Conference 1968: Resolutions and Reports* (London: SPCK; New York: Seabury Press, 1968), p. 138.

The principle of *constitutionality* means that the scope and limits of authority are laid down, agreed and acknowledged. Structures of authority need to embody checks and balances. Limits on authority serve the interests of those who are subject to that authority. Constitutionality is a bulwark against overweening authority. A primary responsibility of a bishop is to uphold the constitution of his or her church and diocese.

The principle of *representation* means that the authority of the whole body is exercised through its appointed representatives, since all the members of the body cannot physically come together for that purpose. They participate through their elected representatives. When bishops seek to work with elected representatives of the clergy and laity they are giving respect to the body of Christ.

The principle of *consent* means that those who are governed must agree to how they are governed and to have a say in it. Authority is constrained by the need to obtain, in general, the consent of those subject to that authority. Laws that lack general acceptance or consensus lose credibility and ultimately lack legitimacy. When rule is resisted by most of its subjects it is regarded as tyranny. Authority has to carry conviction and be persuasive if it is to be effective. The conciliar principle of consent drives the quest for consensus. The consent of the clergy and laity of a diocese is a condition of the effective exercise of authority by the bishop.

Anglican conciliarity

The conciliar dimension of the Christian Church is expressed in the structures both of the Anglican Communion and of its individual member churches.[26] Anglicanism embraces the conciliar dimension

26. For conciliarity in the Church of England see C. J. Podmore, 'The History and Principles of Synodical Government in the Church of England', in A. Melloni and S. Scatena (eds), *Synod and Synodality: Theology, History, Canon Law and Ecumenism in New Contact; International Colloquium Bruges 2003* (John XXIII Foundation for Religious Studies, Bologna; Münster: LIT Verlag, 2005), pp. 213–236. For significant differences of polity within the Communion see C. J. Podmore, 'A Tale of Two Churches: The Ecclesiologies of the Episcopal

that belongs to the very nature of the Church of Christ. It is an inheritor of the history and principles of the late mediaeval conciliar movement, which was stimulated by the trauma of the Great Schism of the West in 1378 when the papacy fragmented, as these ideas were further shaped by the Reformation. Conciliarism at the Anglican Communion level is embodied in the Instruments of Communion: the Lambeth Conference, the Primates Meeting, the Anglican Consultative Council and the ministry of the Archbishop of Canterbury, presiding, moderating and leading in all three.[27]

Conciliarism was not only concerned with General Councils, but picked up the early mediaeval precedent of regional and national councils that had fallen into disuse. Accordingly, Anglican churches have structures of representative government at all appropriate levels. These vary according to the polity of the individual church, but typically would include deanery, diocesan and national synods. Anglicanism gives a voice in these councils to laity and clergy, as well as to bishops. In the General Synod of the Church of England, for example, the House of Bishops has a special responsibility for doctrine, liturgy and ministry, but the House is required to seek the consent of the Houses of Clergy and Laity, listens to what they have to say and endeavours to promote consensus within the Synod. Each House has an effective veto when the Synod is voting by Houses.[28] This offers a picture of the role of the episcopate in listening, reflecting, teaching, guiding and receiving feedback.

Church and the Church of England Compared', *Ecclesiastical Law Journal*, 10 (2008), pp. 34–70; reprinted with minor changes, *International Journal for the Study of the Christian Church*, 8 (2008), pp. 124–154. For a comparative study see N. Doe, *Canon Law in the Anglican Communion* (Oxford: Clarendon Press, 1998). The codes of canon law of the member Churches of the Anglican Communion have been collated in *The Principles of Canon Law Common to the Churches of the Anglican Communion* (London: Anglican Communion Office, 2008).

27. On Anglicanism within the conciliar tradition see Paul Valliere, *Conciliarism: A History of Decision-Making in the Church* (Cambridge: Cambridge University Press, 2012).

28. For a critique of recent practice see Mark Chapman, 'Does the Church of England Have a Theology of General Synod?', *Journal of Anglican Studies*, 11.1 (2013), pp. 15–31.

Theological foundations

Anglicanism grounds conciliarity on baptism as the foundational
sacrament of Christian initiation. Following the Reformers and in
agreement with the teaching of the Second Vatican Council, Anglicans
affirm that, by virtue of their baptism, all Christians are incorporated
into Jesus Christ's threefold messianic identity as prophet, priest and
king.[29] But Anglicans go further than Vatican II explicitly did, in
affirming that, by their participation in this royal priesthood, all the
baptized are mandated to play their part in the governance of Christ's
kingdom. The 1988 Lambeth Conference affirmed that baptism into
the royal priesthood is the foundation of all Christian ministry, lay
and ordained.[30] It is the royal priesthood of the baptized that makes
it right in principle for lay people to participate, in a way appropriate
to their calling, in councils and synods. When bishops work with laity
in the governance and leadership of the diocese, they are doing so not
for pragmatic reasons, for example because lay people pay the bills, but
because they are crowned by Christ in baptism to share in his regal
office.[31]

The conciliar approach to authority can be seen as a development
of the Pauline understanding of the Church as the Body of Christ. The
body metaphor is both *mystical* (linked with the metaphor of the Bride
of Christ and the indwelling of the Holy Spirit) and *political* (as a visible,
ordered community, the Church has various structures of governance
and of oversight that can be interpreted by means of political theory).
Within the range of political options that are available within the
Church's long tradition, Anglicanism is evidently an expression of
reformed, conciliar Catholicism. Its theologians have consistently
appealed to conciliar principles. The conciliar character of Anglicanism
applies both to the Communion as a whole and to each of the member
Churches, since communion (*koinonia*) is an essentially ecclesial
concept. Wherever the Church is found, communion belongs to its
nature, and one key expression of communion is conciliarity. However,
in a plural and divided worldwide Christian Church conciliar authority

29. *Lumen Gentium*, §10–12.

30. *The Truth Shall Make You Free: The Lambeth Conference 1988* (London:
Church House Publishing for the Anglican Consultative Council, 1988), p. 51.

31. On the threefold messianic identity and the royal priesthood see further
Paul Avis, *A Ministry Shaped by Mission* (London and New York: T&T Clark,
2005).

is fragmented and dissipated. In divided Christianity conciliarity is located *within*, rather than *between* each church. This fact makes it all the more important that each church should model practices of discernment that are worthy of Christ, giving priority in their conciliar processes to listening, dialogue and discernment. The current emphasis in the Communion as a whole and in some member churches is very much on this approach. For example, large parts of the agenda of the Church of England's General Synod are given to Bible study, prayer and worship and the whole synodical programme revolves around the celebration of the Eucharist. A synod, like any council, is a Eucharistic event and an expression of Eucharistic communion, with the bishops as the principal ministers of the sacrament.

Chapter 4

THE BISHOP IN LEADERSHIP

A great bandwagon has been rolling by for some years now. Its name is 'leadership' – leadership in industry, in commerce, in the military and in the Church's mission. In magazines acres of print are devoted to the subject. Bookstalls are stocked with an array of leadership titles. In ministerial training there is a heightened emphasis on leadership. Some of this material is sound and helpful. But all too often the idea of leadership that is deployed is an uncritical, naive one, drawn from the world of business and secular organizations. The dominant paradigm in this pervasive discourse is, as Martyn Percy suggests, 'managerially led missiology', one that is 'deeply in thrall to the formulaic', as though the secret of leadership could be defined in a few catch-phrases.[1] The rhetoric of leadership has almost taken over Christian literature about ministry and mission. Notions of leadership derived from organizational or management studies or social psychology threaten to displace ecclesiological reflection on the Christian ministry. These disciplines have their uses and are not to be despised, but they can hardly replace theology.[2]

A lot of 'leadership' material – publications, conferences, seminars and courses – plays into forms of Christian community that have a pragmatic and functional understanding of ministry and ordination, rather than one that is ontological or sacramental. The inflated rhetoric of leadership that we find in these circles tends to borrow

1. Martyn Percy, *Anglicanism: Confidence, Commitment and Communion* (Farnham and Burlington, VT: Ashgate, 2013), p. 7; Martyn Percy, 'Engagement, Diversity, and Distinctiveness: Anglicanism in Contemporary Culture', in Martyn Percy and Robert Boak Slocum (eds), *A Point of Balance: The Weight and Measures of Anglicanism* (New York: Morehouse; Norwich: Canterbury Press, 2013), pp. 13–27 at p. 16.

2. Cf. Paul Avis, *Authority, Leadership and Conflict in the Church* (London: Mowbray, 1992).

wholesale and largely uncritically from modern management and self-realization techniques, as though mere 'leadership' were the answer to all our problems. In fact 'leadership' is not in itself a good thing. It is intrinsically ambiguous – at best a neutral concept that can be put to good or evil, salutary or destructive uses. A leader like Moses, fallible though he was, can guide the people to the Promised Land. A leader like Hitler (Fuhrer = leader), who would brook no contradiction, can plunge his people and the whole world into catastrophe.

The clamour – not least in the Church – for 'strong' leadership is misguided. The cult of the strong leader is dangerous and often disastrous, and that is easily demonstrated.[3] Pope Francis is modelling a different form of leadership, not heroic, not messianic, not going it alone, but a style of leadership that is infused with humility, homely wisdom, spiritual discernment, tact, affirmation of individuals and humour.[4] We are driven to reflect on leadership by the nature of today's world. We cannot command, we cannot direct – in that sense, as Hannah Arendt claimed, 'authority has vanished from the modern world'[5] – but we can offer to lead and to show the way. Leadership is the form that authority takes in a voluntary society such as the Church.

A biblical basis for leadership

It may seem, at first sight, that the biblical grounding for our ideas of 'leadership' is rather thin and that the New Testament material on ministry in the Church points in other directions – towards spiritual gifts, apostolic commissioning and the emergence of distinct offices in the later strands. But there is actually a significant, though limited basis for 'leadership' discourse in the Bible. Clearly there is much about God's leadership of Israel in the Old Testament. The Hebrew Bible has an extensive vocabulary to describe the way that Yahweh has led, still leads and will lead his people, as a nation, as well as individuals among

3. Archie Brown, *The Myth of the Strong Leader: Political Leadership in Modern Politics* (New York: Random House, Basic Books, 2014).

4. See, for a semi-popular presentation, Chris Lowney, *Pope Francis: Why He Leads the Way He Leads – Lessons from the First Jesuit Pope* (Chicago: Loyola Press, 2013).

5. Hannah Arendt (ed.), 'What Is Authority?', *Between Past and Future* (Harmondsworth: Penguin, 1977), pp. 9–10.

them, to salvation. A cluster of overlapping verbs evokes rich nuances in the idea of leadership.[6] Perhaps the dominant image is of the LORD as the Shepherd of his people (e.g. Genesis 48.15; Psalms 23.1; 74.1; 95.7; Isaiah 40.11; Jeremiah 23.1–4; Ezekiel 34).

The New Testament picks up the Hebrew Bible's image of the Good Shepherd leading and caring for his flock. This image is perhaps the primary scriptural source for the concept of divine leadership. John chapter 10 is the key: 'He calls his own sheep by name and leads (*exagei*) them out' (v. 3). Many a sermon has pointed out that, in the Holy Land, it was – and perhaps still is – the practice for the shepherd to lead the flock from the front, rather than driving them from behind, as farmers do in some other cultures. Interestingly, the local shepherd who grazes his sheep on my fields at home in Devon, England, leads them from the front to pastures new – but his old dad is in a van, chivvying them along from the rear! As Jesus says in John 10, 'When he has brought out all his own, he goes ahead of them, and the sheep follow him because they know his voice' (v. 4). There is an echo of the Good Shepherd imagery in Revelation 7.17: 'for the Lamb at the centre of the throne will be their shepherd, and he will guide (*hodegesei*, to lead the way) them to springs of the water of life' (echoing Psalm 23.2 and Isaiah 49.10).

Divine leading is clearly strongly represented in both Testaments, but the crucial issue for us is whether there is a biblical basis for human leadership in the Church. The theological tradition of the royal priesthood of the baptized that runs from 1 Peter 2, through Calvin, to Newman, holds that Christ's messianic (anointed) identity as Prophet, Priest and King is bestowed on his people: they are incorporated into his corporate *persona* through baptism.[7] Therefore, because Jesus Christ

---

6. Psalm 25.5: 'Lead me in your truth and teach me, for you are the God of my salvation.' Isaiah 42.16: 'I will lead the blind by a road they do not know.' Here the verb translated in English 'lead' is *darak*, to cause to tread. Isaiah 42.21: 'They did not thirst when he led them through the deserts.' Here the verb is *yalak*, to cause to go on. Psalm 80.1: '... you who lead Joseph like a flock.' Here the verb is *nahag*, to lead or drive. Psalm 5.8: 'Lead me, O LORD, in your righteousness ... make your way straight before my path.' Here the verb is *nachah*, to lead forth.

7. Biblical material in Paul Avis, *A Ministry Shaped by Mission* (London and New York: T&T Clark, 2005), pp. 65–69; historical material in Paul Avis *Beyond the Reformation? Authority, Primacy and Unity in the Conciliar Tradition* (London and New York: T&T Clark, 2006), pp. 5–12. See also Calvin, *Institutes*

is the Good Shepherd, he exercises his care of the flock through human under-shepherds; if he leads and guides his people like a flock, he does so through the instrumentality of those who are called to leadership and pastoral care. In the Old Testament a variety of leaders are described as shepherds to whom Yahweh entrusts the care of his flock. In particular, David serves as the model for the promised messianic shepherd-king (Ezekiel 37.24; Micah 5.2–4).

The image of the Good Shepherd is applied in a derived and secondary way to the pastors of the Church in 1 Peter 5.1–4:

> Now as an elder myself (*sumpresbuteros*)…I exhort the elders (*presbuterous*) among you to tend the flock of God that is in your charge, exercising the oversight (*episkopountes*)…be examples to the flock. And when the chief shepherd (*archipoimen*) appears, you will win the crown of glory…

Here the pastorate of Jesus Christ is shared with and exercised through the under-shepherds of his Church.[8]

Luke uses the term 'leader' (*hegoumenos*) three times in his two books, the Gospel and the Acts. In Luke 22.26 – a unique use of leadership language in the Gospels – Jesus says that the one who is a leader (*ho hegoumenos*) among the disciples should be as the one who serves (*ho diakonon*). In the Acts of the Apostles the term is used metaphorically. In Acts 14.12 Paul, mistaken for Hermes, is described as 'the leader of the word' or chief speaker (*hegoumenos tou legou*). In Acts 15.22 two men are designated to be companions of Paul and Barnabas; they are described as 'leading men among the brethren' (*andras hegoumenous en tois adelphois*).

The term *hegoumenoi* is used in classical Greek for persons in various positions of authority in provinces, towns, cities, communities

---

of the Christian Religion, trans. Henry Beveridge (London: James Clarke, 1962), vol. 2, pp. 425–432 (II, xv); J. H. Newman, *The Via Media of the Anglican Church*, ed. H. D. Weidner (Oxford: Clarendon Press, 1990), pp. 24–26 (a republication of Newman's Anglican work *The Prophetical Office of the Church*, with a new Preface).

8. What is not – and cannot be – shared is the unique 'leadership' of Christ as *archēgos* – the leader, prince, author or pioneer of life and salvation in Acts 3.15; 5.31 (cf. Hebrews 12.2); see C. K. Barrett, *The Acts of the Apostles* (ICC, London and New York: T&T Clark, 1994), vol. 1, pp. 197–198, 290–291.

and associations. In both classical and New Testament Greek it is a generic term for those who rule or lead and does not imply that they hold any specific office. The substantive is *hegoumenos*, ruler, leader. The verb is *hegeomai*, to lead, to guide, to go before, to rule, to be a leader (or – its commonest use in the New Testament – to think, to consider). Although Paul does not use this particular word, his letters testify to the reality of leadership roles in the congregation. Subsequent to its use in Hebrews, the Christian use of *hegoumenoi* seems to be associated with the church in Rome (as we see in 1 Clement and *The Shepherd of Hermas*) and we might conjecture that this fact may be related to the comparatively late emergence of monarchical episcopacy in that city.

It is in the Epistle to the Hebrews,[9] and at the very end of that letter, that we find the most explicit references to leaders in the Church: 'remember your leaders'; 'obey your leaders'; 'greet your leaders'. (The NRSV and the REB translate *hegoumenoi* as 'leaders', while the KJB/AV has 'them which have the rule over you' and Tyndale has 'them which have the oversight of you'.) We turn to these key passages in slightly more detail.

Hebrews 13.7: 'Remember your leaders (*hegoumenoi*), those who spoke the word of God to you; consider the outcome of their way of life and imitate their faith.' These leaders are identified with the preaching of the word. They have probably now died, but their example and teaching deserve to be held in remembrance. We do not need to assume that they were martyred, though Calvin interprets it in that sense: 'those who had sealed with their own blood the teachings handed on by them'.[10] The imperative is in the

<hr/>

9. Resources for these interpretations include: Friedrich Büchsal, in G. Kittel (ed.), G. W. Bromiley (trans.), *Theological Dictionary of the New Testament* (Grand Rapids: Eerdmans, 1964), vol. 2, p. 907; Craig R. Koester, *Hebrews*, Anchor Bible (New York: Doubleday, 2001); William L. Lane, *Hebrews 9–13*, Word Bible Commentary (Dallas, TX: Word Books, 1991); F. F. Bruce, *The Epistle to the Hebrews*, New International Commentary on the New Testament (Grand Rapids: Eerdmans, 1964).

10. John Calvin, *The Epistle of Paul the Apostle to the Hebrews and the First and Second Epistles of St Peter, Calvin's Commentaries*, eds. David W. Torrance and Thomas F. Torrance, William B. Johnston (trans.) (Edinburgh: Oliver and Boyd, 1963), p. 207.

present tense: 'continue to remember'. Why is this verse followed immediately by 'Jesus Christ is the same yesterday, today and forever'? Is it meant as an antidote to the human weaknesses of the leaders ('Remember your leaders, but above all remember that Jesus Christ will never let you down')? Or – more satisfactorily in my opinion – is it filling out the content of the word of God that the leaders had brought to the recipients of the letter ('Remember your leaders who brought you the message of the unchanging love and power of Jesus Christ')? That interpretation brings out the continuity of the discourse.

Hebrews 13.17 deals with how these Hebrew Christians are to regard their present, living leaders: 'Obey [present imperative: "continue to obey"] your leaders and submit to them for they are keeping watch ["sleepless vigil"] over your souls and will give an account [to God].' The leaders are entitled to obedience as those who preach and teach the word of God and exercise oversight in the Church. The power of the word lent them their authority. They may well have literally lost sleep because of their responsibilities.

Hebrews 13.24 gives another insight into the nature of leadership in the early Church: 'Greet all your leaders and all the saints.' There was a plurality of leaders; they were distinguished from the rest of the community and they were the first to be greeted on behalf of the author of the epistle, but not at the expense of the faithful, who are described as saints (*tous hagious*). It seems clear that Hebrews reflects a situation in which there was a plurality of leaders, rather than one overall pastor or bishop. The privileges of all Christians are emphasized: the whole community may have boldness to approach the throne of grace (4.16); it is expected that teachers will emerge from the community (5.12); and everyone will have to give an account to God (4.13). On the other hand, Hebrews does not indicate that there was the sort of spontaneous charismatic worship that we find described in 1 Corinthians. There is stability and effective oversight, but differentiated orders – e.g. bishop, priest, deacon – have not yet emerged.

How should we relate this biblical material on leadership to the mission and ministry of the Church? As we have seen, the tasks of the Church are to teach, to sanctify and to govern: to teach the faith and proclaim the gospel; to sanctify or make holy through worship and the sacraments; to govern through pastoral care and oversight. This triple task comprises the essential mission of the Church. The tasks can be broadly correlated, in reverse order, with the Great Commission of Matthew 28.16–20: to make disciples, to baptize and to teach. The tasks are given to the apostolic community as a body, so that (as Vatican II says, LG 10–12) every believer, baptized into Christ's messianic mission, is called to play their part in carrying out these three tasks (*munera*).

Within the royal, prophetic priesthood that comprises the whole Church of Christ (1 Peter 2.4–10), the tasks of teaching, sanctifying and governing are exercised in a particular way by bishops and priests, with deacons assisting. The ministry of the ordained is representative in a twofold way: representative of the Church that is the Body of Christ, and representative of Christ as Head of the Body. The clergy are called, commissioned, gifted, given authority and placed under oversight (in shorthand, ordained) for that role.

It is these tasks that are the key modes of leadership. Bishops lead by doing in an appropriate way precisely what the Church does, exactly what the Church is here for: teaching and proclaiming the gospel; facilitating worship and celebrating the sacraments; governing and guiding, as far as possible in accord with the whole community. Leadership cannot be anything other than carrying out the tasks that the Church is called to fulfil. Leadership is not a flamboyant display of personality or of individual gifts and talents; nor is it the sort of ego-trip where we present our own spiritual experience to others as an example and inspiration. Leadership in the Church consists in the faithful, disciplined, skilled carrying out of precisely the commissioned tasks of the Church – teaching, sanctifying and governing – in such a way that we support, encourage, inspire and guide the people of God committed to our care so that they are able to realize their own calling from God to the fullest extent possible.

Strategic communication

Christian leadership almost always involves leadership from the Church to the Church: it is an 'internal' conversation, leaders and led both being within the restricted circle of the Church. But, thanks to electronic communication, bishops will also find themselves addressing, whether they like it or not, a wider audience beyond the Church. Even when bishops think that they are addressing the faithful, their words are overheard by other constituencies: people of goodwill on the fringe of the Christian community; people now beyond the Church who are disillusioned with it and wanting to find fault; politicians looking for an opportunity to use the Church to their advantage; and the media searching for a story of conflict or scandal. This diverse audience is almost completely unquantifiable: its complexion is largely unknown and its size cannot be reliably measured; it has no boundaries and cannot be managed or controlled. Given those conditions, bishops individually and collectively will aim to direct their message, as far as possible, in a strategic way to every level of society: the level of the state and public policy; within civil society, that is to say from one institution to others; and in the local community made up of neighbourhoods and local networks. Even leadership initiatives that are meant to be purely internal to the Church and are not overtly directed towards the wider community will be overheard, picked up and run away with. Today it is not possible to set boundaries to Christian leadership. In terms of leadership, the famous words of the founders of Methodist evangelism, George Whitefield and John Wesley, 'I take the whole world as my parish', now have a rather ironic ring. The world is our parish, whether we like it or not. The opportunities that the mass media offer to bishops are such that it is vital to approach issues of communication in a thought-out and strategic way.

Instant electronic communication and (dependent on this) the mass media are the ever-present context of Christian leadership.[11] Bishops can find themselves speaking into the media maelstrom. They need to be acutely aware that even the more respectable forms of mass media live by lies, in the sense of – at the least – being 'economical with the truth', presenting a selective and partial account of events and statements and promoting their ideology. They must be cultivating their ratings by 'playing to the gallery', giving their readers what they want to hear, for they understand their audience better than their audience understands itself. Whatever the media seizes on will inevitably be distorted. So bishops need to be constantly aware of media exposure, to have good advice available about how to handle it, but also to be able to take the opportunities that it offers. Without the media and electronic communication bishops can address only a fairly intimate audience; they are talking in a corner of the room. With the aid of the media leaders can project their message widely, throughout 'many mansions'.

So bishops (like politicians) should be wary of courting the media – they cannot control it. Those who live by the media will die by the media. Bishops speak into a void and cannot tell what echoes will return. To

11. Cf. Wesley Carr, *Ministry and the Media* (London: SPCK, 1990) – a pre-world wide web discussion.

borrow the title of one of R. S. Thomas's volumes of poems, 'the echoes return slow': bishops' words and deeds can continue to reverberate long after the bishop thinks that she/he has moved on. But on the other hand, at times the echoes can return all too quickly! Like a game of Chinese whispers, what comes back is likely to be very different from what the bishop actually said and intended. Therefore, bishops need to be bold without being impulsive; they need to weigh their words, but not to be inhibited; and they need to remember that many people within and beyond the Church long simply to hear the fundamental truths of the Christian faith spoken by Christian leaders. Bishops should not be embarrassed to speak plainly of the love of God in Jesus Christ; of the wonderful message of the Gospels; of saving faith and Christian commitment; of the precious gift of baptism, the strengthening power of confirmation and the privilege of Holy Communion; of the joy of the consecrated Christian life. Above all they should hold up Jesus Christ so that others may see him – perhaps for the first time – with the eyes of faith. These themes are not what most bishops are heard to be talking about – and that is not entirely the fault of selective reporting.

The bishop as manager?

Although, as we have said earlier, bishops are not CEOs, effective leadership requires a modicum of management skills. But first and foremost, leadership needs to be distinguished from management. In some institutions, including the Church, management is often confused with leadership or offered as a substitute for it. But managers cannot fulfil the role of leaders and any bishop who sees him- or herself primarily as a manager will not be able to give effective leadership. Management in the wrong place is simply surrogate leadership. The manager-bishop is frankly in the wrong job.

There are certain rare individuals, such as F. D. Roosevelt or Winston Churchill, who are outstanding leaders, especially in times of grave crisis, but who are not interested in management and lack the skills for it. They rely on others to pick up the pieces, as it were, of management. A senior official in the Church of England, who served bishops and archbishops, compared himself to the man who used to follow the horse and cart along the road with a bucket and shovel to clear up the mess they left behind. For many individuals, however, leadership is built on a foundation of sound management skills. These include an orderly approach to work (tidy administration), an understanding of how the organization or institution works (the purpose for which it exists and how its structures mesh together), the ability to prioritize tasks, to collaborate with colleagues and to delegate responsibility. Even so, these management gifts alone are not enough to constitute leadership.

Let us try to identify the essentials of management, as distinct from leadership. Management is concerned with the efficient and effective deployment of resources in fulfilling the tasks demanded by the overall goals of the organization or institution. Managers alone do not set the goals of the organization, though they sometimes imagine that they do. These goals are already given, engraved in the DNA of the institution; they simply need to be discovered. They are inherent in the origin, tradition and structure of the institution and together constitute its *raison d'être*, its mission. The goals are reshaped and articulated in fresh ways by those who have the responsibility and authority to do so – the leaders of the organization. Managers have the job of implementing the vision given by the leadership of the organization or institution. They do this by the way that they use the human, material and financial resources that they are able to deploy. Their skills are in prioritizing needs, gathering and distributing resources and problem solving with regard to connecting resources to goals.

Although management cannot substitute for leadership, managers also require a necessary modicum of leadership skills, because a key part of their role is to maintain morale, to motivate individuals, to galvanize the workforce in the performance of its tasks, so that each employee gives of their best and each team or group of employees works efficiently. A good manager is able to bring the best out of those that he or she works with, while keeping them directed towards the given task. The Church looks to the bishop and the clergy for this vital role. Bishops who recognize both the importance of sound management and the fact that they are not equipped to undertake management themselves will consciously look to their close colleagues, the archdeacons and diocesan executive officers, to fulfil this role.

Individuals within an organization find motivation through a sense that they and their work are valued. Value accrues mainly through a perception of the worth of the task being performed, augmented by material rewards. Enhanced material rewards in the form of pay, holiday, hours worked and ancillary benefits can partly redress any tedium, frustration or exhaustion inherent in the work as it is done. But because of a lack of resources, the Church can only provide these kinds of rewards for its clergy to a very limited extent. On the other hand, the value of the work to the mission of the organization can help to compensate for poor material rewards by enhancing a sense of purpose, value and self-esteem, and this is the main avenue of encouragement that is open to bishops with regard to their clergy: reward all participation and doubly reward exceptional contributions.

The bishop as leader

Leadership can be defined as the capacity first to attract fellow workers and then to motivate them in task performance. Leadership depends on authority and is therefore implicated in power play. But leadership cannot neglect management issues or ignore the managers themselves because it must necessarily work with whatever resources management can put in place in support of the leaders' vision. Leadership therefore has a unitive, integrating function, holding various groups and their energies together in a common cause. Leadership in the diocese sets the bishop at the centre of a nexus of activity and of working relationships. The bishop cannot control this dynamic and should have no desire to do so, but the bishop can inspire, enable, inform, guide and, if necessary, restrain.

Leaders (in our case, bishops) are servants and agents of the institution, not freelance individuals, still less spiritual virtuosi. They are shackled to the institution, which is the organization seen in its enduring, historic mode. They are necessarily constrained by that fact, though they can help to reshape the institution somewhat. In order to work effectively within their institution leaders need to understand the nature of institutions as such: that they are made by history and tradition; that they gain energy by interacting with other institutions in civil society; that they embody a set of moral values that guide the members in their behaviour towards one another and towards those outside; that they depend on many individuals and groups pulling their weight in a co-ordinated way; that they receive rather than invent their mission; and that they perpetuate themselves into the future in the service of that mission. That is something of what it means to serve an institution, even if – or especially if – it happens to be our own branch of the Christian Church.

So bishops need a profound 'sense of the Church' – of its unity, holiness, catholicity and apostolicity. This 'sense of the Church' comes through soaking up the Scriptures, through deep study of the Christian tradition and through surrender to the liturgy as it is celebrated. Bishops need to be focused on the Church's triple God-given task – making the word of God known through preaching, teaching and other forms of witness; celebrating the sacraments of Christian initiation and the Eucharist; and providing pastoral care and oversight to all who will receive them. Bishops need to be biblical scholars; they need to be ecclesiologists; and they need to be missiologists as well. Their expertise in these areas, combined with the platform that their office gives them and the personal qualities of character and life that will win them respect, will ensure that they have a receptive audience. Where they do not have expertise of their own – perhaps in the study of social and cultural trends that provide the context for the Church's mission ('reading the signs of the times') – they will need to ensure that they carve out time for reading and receive expert advice.

The bishop's role in leadership is vital, irreplaceable. Without leadership any institution drifts aimlessly. It suffers entropy: its energies run down, it loses direction, the vision fades and the goals become opaque. What leaders can do is to refresh or burnish the vision: inspire, enable, inform and guide the community in the service of its given purpose. Through their well-chosen words, strategic actions and personal example, leaders act as a catalyst for the organization. They can give hope that people's labour is not in vain; they can quicken the energies of their fellow workers with a fresh sense of purpose.

Rhetoric and mere assertion will not achieve this and will be regarded as so much hot air. Mere bookish (or these days far less than bookish) musings will not do the business either. But coolly passionate reasoning, grounded in knowledge, and moving to a conclusion, will surely convince and mobilize people. Leaders need to make their case by elaborating arguments, supported by information, by facts. In that way they give respect to their hearers and on the basis of respect seek to convince their judgement. *Reasoned persuasion* is the key to moving people forward and this implies exceptional intellectual ability.

But what sort of vision can a bishop bring? The vision that sustains the Church is a biblical, theological and moral vision of human wholeness, flourishing and ultimate fulfilment in union with God the Holy Trinity. That vision is shot through with adoration and is expressed definitively in worship. The overarching idea of the Christian vision is the Kingdom or Reign of God announced by Jesus Christ and embodied in his person and work. Part of the bishop's calling as a teacher of Christian truth is to find the words to articulate that vision in a way that inspires and motivates believers and attracts those who do not yet have a fully formed faith but are open to the Christian message – and, of course, to validate their words by their deeds and life.

While all leaders are constrained by the institution, which was there long before them and will probably continue on its way long after they are gone, they are not at its mercy. In conjunction with managers, they can play a key role in the ongoing reform of the structures and working methods of the institution. Without continuous reform, the institution will decline in effectiveness. But attempts at reform need to be deeply informed by a sense of the history, purpose and make-up of the institution and this is where specialized knowledge and expertise come into play. In the case of bishops, what is particularly needed at this point is expertise in Scripture, theology, liturgy and Church history. The Reformation slogan *ecclesia reformata semper reformanda* (the reformed church is always reforming) points to an insight that affects not only the Church, but all historic institutions. As they pass through time their energy and efficiency will reduce unless they are renewed to meet fresh challenges. In the case of the Church a diminution of spiritual efficiency and spiritual energy means a lowering of standards of holiness and lessening of zeal for mission and evangelism.

Reform and renewal are an ever-present need of the Church; reform is perpetual by definition.[12] Sometimes the Church longs desperately for reform, as much of the Western Church did in the late Middle Ages and as many in the Roman Catholic Church did before Pope Francis was elected. Historically, reform has meant rectifying bad pastoral practice (abuses), reconstructing the way that the Church was organized, restoring the fabric of visible unity and refocusing on the gospel and the saving work of Christ. Reform goes hand in hand with repentance and conversion and results in fresh spiritual energies.

We tend to associate 'reformation' with the sixteenth century, but the theme is patristic – indeed biblical – in origin.[13] The need for reform

12. John P. Bradbury, *Perpetually Reforming: A Theology of Church Renewal and Reform* (London and New York: Bloomsbury, T&T Clark, 2013).

13. Gerhart Ladner, *The Idea of Reform: Its Impact on Christian Thought and Action in the Age of the Fathers* (Cambridge, MA: Harvard University Press, 1959); Christopher M. Bellito and David Zachariah Flanagan (eds), *Reassessing Reform: A Historical Investigation into Church Renewal* (Washington, DC: The Catholic University of America Press, 2012).

was embraced by the Second Vatican Council and expounded by Yves Congar, Karl Rahner and Hans Küng.[14] So the imperative of reform does not belong only to those who bear the name 'Reformed'; it can make itself felt in surprising places, as agents of reform are raised up by God when they are most needed.

When is reform authentic and when is it merely a veneer put on changes that have been made for dubious political or ideological reasons? The word 'reform' has long been highjacked by politicians to justify pragmatic, partisan policies, from budget cuts to meddling with the constitution. The sixteenth-century Reformers used the criteria of true proclamation of the gospel and right administration of the sacraments to guide the reform process. In other words, true reform lifts up Jesus Christ and brings the gospel freshly to light. The Reformation was also imbued with a strong moral imperative – seeking the purity and holiness of the Church. Faith and life go together in the ongoing reform of the Church.

Leaders are made, not born

The extensive scholarly literature about leadership is quite clear that leaders are made, not born. Leadership skills are elicited by the challenge of the situation when it is met with the right character and aptitudes. Leadership is not particularly about charisma, but it is about character and it is about skills. Winston Churchill is widely regarded as an outstanding wartime leader of the United Kingdom and the free world. But in the years leading up to 1940 Churchill was a diminished, careworn figure, widely mistrusted and seemingly defeated. The call to office and to national and international leadership galvanized him. He saw his whole previous life as 'a walk with destiny' to that moment. As a matter of fact, natural energies and capacities are not the most important qualities that are to be looked for in the potential leader, and overweening ambition in that direction is to be distrusted. Much more significant is profound strength of character and solid integrity. Of course, not everyone has suitable aptitudes that can be drawn out, and some individuals seem endowed by nature with striking attributes so that they stand head and shoulders above their fellows; but even these natural gifts need to be shaped by education and training to serve the cause of leadership. The key to leadership is *formation* – formation

14. See Avis, *Beyond the Reformation?*, chapter 13.

within a total environment that is conductive to the emergence of salutary leadership.[15]

So there is a sense in which the bishop's leadership is formed by his or her reception in the community; leadership cannot be imposed 'from above'. Because leadership requires the free consent and support of followers, and a leader is nothing without followers, it can only be given, not assumed. Leadership emerges when there is the right combination of character, aptitude and opportunity. The call to serve in a leadership role is the critical factor in the making of a leader. In Christianity, that call comes from God and the Church working in harmony (we trust). Bishops will be sustained through thick and thin by their sense of call, from God and the Church, and the affirmation that it brings.

Leadership functions at the level of symbolism, not literalism; it works obliquely. The apt word and the telling gesture need to be projected into the public arena. A leader of a large institution cannot communicate directly with the majority of his or her constituent members, or be known personally to most of them – and this is particularly true of the Church, which is a widely dispersed community. But what the members hear and see of their leader's words and actions should resonate with many of them with a sense that it is precisely what is called for in the circumstances – just what is needed ('That was so apt.'). Of course, individuals will not all agree about the appropriateness of the bishop's words and deeds, but this does not represent failure on the part of the leader – it could not be otherwise. But the leader has achieved something worthwhile if his or her auditors are caused to *engage* with what has been said or done, rather than brushing it aside as irrelevant or simply inadequate to the occasion. At the very least, it is worthy of their attention. When that is secured, there is more to play for.

Because leadership is awarded by others and depends on freely given assent – not least in the Church – it is always accountable. However long the piece of string, one end is always held by the community of followers: leaders must be alert to the tug of the string. Accountability can take various forms and be mediated by various structures, but it is a two-way traffic and its essence is mutual trust. On the part of the

15. This is the thrust of an exceptionally useful account: Simon Western, *Leadership: A Critical Text* (London: Sage, 2008). The formation model is dubbed by Western 'Eco-leadership' because of its vital connection to the conducive environment, and is distinguished from 'controlling', 'therapeutic' and 'messianic' models of leadership.

leader it takes the form of a sense of responsibility for the role that has been entrusted to them by the community. On the part of the followers it takes the form of expectations that may or may not be met. When those expectations are met to a sufficient extent, the leader is rewarded, so to speak, with the commitment of the followers. But the trust placed in leaders can always be withdrawn, even if those persons continue in office and outward appearances remain the same. Then we have a loss of confidence or a breakdown of trust between the leader and the led, and followers will begin to look for a new leader. So as leaders we cannot rest on our laurels. Our leadership skills need to be constantly refreshed, constantly reburnished.

Chapter 5

THE BISHOP IN COLLABORATIVE MINISTRY

Collaborative ministry is an absolutely vital dimension of episcopal ministry in today's Church. How a bishop handles questions of collaboration, team work and delegation can make or break that bishop's episcopate. The context for the issue of collaborative ministry is the mission of all baptized Christians, the Church as the living body of Christ, within which individuals are called by the Holy Spirit through the Church to many diverse ministries. The bishop has a key role in calling out, or eliciting these ministries and then knitting them together into a coherent whole, working towards a common goal. Since, in many dioceses, it is not possible for the bishop to relate directly to every individual minister in his or her diocese, this integrating role is carried through the bishop's example, direction and teaching. In this context the bishop is called to *model* collaborative ministry for the ministers of the diocese.

The theological heart of the matter here is episcopal collegiality. In sharp contrast to the Roman Catholic Church, which has produced a wealth of theological reflection on episcopal collegiality since Vatican II, interpreting it by means of the key concept of 'hierarchical communion' – even if its practice falls far short of its theory – the Anglican Communion has scant theological resources on episcopal collegiality.

At the start of his major study of collaborative ministry, Bishop Stephen Pickard writes of his conviction that 'the joy of Christian ministry arises out of collaborative practice where team work, shared ministry and common purpose combine together to further the mission of God in the world.'[1] Pickard notes ruefully, however, that 'the clergy generally evince minimal aptitude for such a way of ministry' and he

---

1. Stephen Pickard, *Theological Foundations for Collaborative Ministry* (Farnham; Burlington, VT: Ashgate, 2009), p. vii.

identifies a 'lack of inner coherence among the ministries' as 'a major cause of conflict and dissipation of energies within churches' (pp. 1, 7).

I share Stephen Pickard's sense that much joy and satisfaction in ministry comes, not from trying to 'go it alone' as the omni-competent, all-wise leader (whose feet of clay eventually and inescapably will be revealed), but rather from a comprehensively collaborative approach. The antithesis to a collaborative approach is the autocratic method, which Pickard sees as an attempt to deal with 'fear and anxiety about loss of control by the exercise of power over others' (p. 2). The clergy – who are often reluctant to delegate and unsure of themselves with regard to sharing responsibility – will learn to put collaborative ministry into practice as they see their bishop modelling it in relation to the bishop's own senior colleagues.

A philosophy of cooperation, collaboration and mutual assistance is intrinsic to Christianity. The gospel implies a preferential option, so to speak, for working together on the part of its ministers, a preferential option that is based, not only on collegiality in a common ministerial calling, but ultimately on our baptismal solidarity in the body of Christ. As Pickard says, 'when the Church acts in a collaborative manner it actualises its own deepest reality', because that is the way 'in which the ministry of the gospel is a gospel ministry' (p. 7). When bishops, who have the highest public profile of all ministers, demonstrate mutual respect among themselves, seek to benefit from one another's wisdom and act in harmony, they give warm encouragement to the faithful who look to them for an example and, at the same time, they effectively commend the faith to those looking on from outside the Church who may come to see the humility and generosity of the bishop as pointers to the character of Christ. When bishops consistently act in this way, not only *vis-à-vis* each other, but also in relation to their closest presbyteral and lay colleagues, the impact is even greater. 'The joy of ministry', says Pickard, 'is rooted in the capacity for collaborative practices that draw the gifts of the body of Christ together and orientate them towards the world' (p. 8).

But a caveat needs to be entered at this point. However strongly the bishop may feel him- or herself being drawn into close collegial relations with clergy, a certain detachment, even distance, must remain. This element of personal space is necessary not for reasons of pride or superiority on the bishop's part, but to enable the bishop to fulfil the exacting legal requirements of clergy discipline when this is called for – and the bishop cannot know in advance where or when discipline may be necessary. Of course, the bishop will turn to his or her legal advisers before taking any steps in a potential disciplinary case, but the need to stand somewhat apart remains. A bishop walks the tightrope between close support and involvement with regard to the clergy, on the one hand, and the objectivity that oversight requires, on the other.

Episcopal collegiality

For a bishop, collaborative ministry primarily takes the form of collegiality with fellow bishops. By virtue of their ordination to the episcopate, bishops are members of an episcopal college. This concept reflects an understanding, mentioned earlier and derived from Cyprian, Bishop of Carthage, martyred in AD 250, of the solidarity of the episcopate as a collective reality in which each bishop has a share. Each episcopally ordered church has its college; more widely, there is an episcopal college of the Anglican Communion and, beyond the immediate bounds of the Communion, a 'wider episcopal fellowship' of the bishops whose churches are in communion with each other.

Ecclesial communion is the foundation of episcopal collegiality and is its *sine qua non*, its essential condition. Episcopal collegiality is predicated on sacramental communion: the college is a Eucharistic reality. Collegiality in the ecclesiological sense does not yet pertain between bishops who are not in sacramental communion with each other, even though they may be on good terms personally and even undertake certain initiatives together, such as public statements, mission projects or training opportunities for clergy and laity. Such instances of good practice certainly foreshadow episcopal collegiality that is based on ecclesial communion and contain intimations of its reality, but nevertheless fall short of the principle of 'bishops in communion', a key building block of episcopally ordered churches and of their connection with each other.

With regard to the 'wider episcopal fellowship', this embodies a broader collegiality with the bishops of Churches in Communion with the whole Anglican Communion (the Old Catholic Churches of the Union of Utrecht, the Mar Thoma Church of South India and the Philippine Independent Church). This dimension of episcopal collegiality comes to realization at the Lambeth Conference and there is considerable untapped potential in this wider episcopal college.

Again, there is a real collegiality between the bishops of certain Anglican Churches and the bishops of those Churches with whom their own churches (but not the whole Communion) are in communion.

This collegiality includes the bishops of The Episcopal Church and the Evangelical Lutheran Church in America (through *Called to Common Mission*); the bishops of the Anglican Church of Canada and the Evangelical Lutheran Church in Canada (through the Waterloo Agreement); and the bishops of the British and Irish Anglican Churches and the Nordic and Baltic Lutheran Churches (through the Porvoo Agreement). This expression of episcopal collegiality within certain global regions has hardly begun to be realized in practice, though a start has been made in all the areas mentioned. Moreover, through the Anglican Communion's ecumenical dialogue with the Roman Catholic Church and the Orthodox Churches, Anglican bishops seek and aspire to a communion and therefore a collegiality that is truly universal. At present, and for the foreseeable future, however, such a universal collegiality is not possible because there is not a relationship of sacramental communion and interchangeable ordained ministry between any of the Churches in ecumenical dialogue (if there were, dialogue would be superseded by formal agreement).

In the Roman Catholic Church sworn obedience to the pope as head of the episcopal college is a condition of membership of the college and collegiality is understood primarily in terms of 'hierarchical communion'. But the college of Anglican bishops is essentially a fellowship of equals. All bishops are seen, on the same level, as successors of the apostles. Within the college, however, some – archbishops, presiding bishops, primuses, moderators – may be called to a role involving a degree of primacy, that is to say (depending on the polity of the church concerned) to preside at general synods and general conventions and at gatherings of bishops, to have metropolitical authority in visitations and to be a resort of appeal in disputes. Anglicans recognize a principle of primacy, as well as a principle of collegiality, but the person exercising primacy in any form is always *primus inter pares*, first among equals.[2]

One rare Anglican discussion of episcopal collegiality is the teaching document of the House of Bishops of the Church of England *Bishops in Communion*.[3] It sets collegiality in the framework of the reality of communion (*koinonia*) in the Church. The communion that the

2. On the Anglican (especially Church of England) understanding of primacy, see Colin Podmore, *Aspects of Anglican Identity* (London: Church House Publishing, 2005).

3. *Bishops in Communion* (London: Church House Publishing, 2001).

Church has received is with God the Holy Trinity: 'our fellowship (*koinonia*) is with the Father and with his Son, Jesus Christ' (1 John 1.3). Like the first disciples, the Church today seeks to 'continue in the apostles' teaching and fellowship (*koinonia*)' (Acts 2.42). St Paul brings out the collaborative nature of *koinonia* when he gives thanks to God for the way that the Philippians have offered a 'sharing [or partnership, *koinonia*] in the gospel from the first day until now' – that is to say, for all the practical support that they had given him to enable him to carry out his apostolic ministry (Philippians 1.5), to the extent that it could be seen as a joint effort.

It is not simply individuals who are 'in communion' with God and with each other; the Church as a body is constituted as a communion through baptism, including the baptismal confession of faith (1 Corinthians 12.13), because the Church as a body is baptized corporately into the death and resurrection of Christ (1 Corinthians 10.1–2; 12.1). The Church is sustained in this communion through the Eucharist, which culminates in Holy Communion, a sacramental participation in the body of Christ (1 Corinthians 10.16–17).

The episcopate has a special role in representing and maintaining the fabric of communion – the unity and continuity of the Church. Bishops do this in three dimensions: personal, collegial and communal – the three dimensions of all ministry that are highlighted in the most widely received ecumenical text, *Baptism, Eucharist and Ministry (BEM)*.[4] How are these three dimensions reflected in the bishop's ministry?

The *personal* dimension relates to the leadership role of the individual bishop and to the truth that Christ ministers in his Church primarily through persons, not through impersonal committees. God did not send a committee to save the world. There is no substitute for personal, face-to-face interaction. Every baptized Christian represents Christ as they go about their daily discipleship, and all the ordained represent him in a more intense and focused way, because they are given authority to speak and act in his name. But the bishop represents Christ in an enhanced way, as someone who has enlarged pastoral responsibilities and is a 'father in God' or a 'mother in God' to laity and clergy alike.

The *collegial* dimension points to the common task of all ministers and particularly to the work of bishops who are called to hold those ministries together, to help to support, enable and focus them. The

---

4. *Baptism, Eucharist and Ministry* (Geneva: World Council of Churches, 1982).

collegial dimension brings out the truth that ministries do not stand alone; they stand together or not at all as different facets of the one ministry of Jesus Christ in and through his body. In the collegial dimension of episcopal ministry, bishops support and encourage one another, take counsel together and accept a measure of collective responsibility – though ultimately the diocesan bishop has an irreducible responsibility. It can be seen at the diocesan level where the diocesan college of bishops (if there are suffragans as well as the diocesan) works as one through close consultation and mutual support (the Diocese of Toronto has practised this kind of collegiality for thirty years and many other dioceses have a similar practice). It operates at the national level in what is variously styled the House of Bishops, the Bishop's Meeting or the Bench of Bishops; and it functions at the global level in the Lambeth Conference.

St Paul speaks of one of his co-workers as 'my loyal yoke fellow' (Philippians 4.3). Paul's practice of collaborative working in the Acts of the Apostles and the way that he speaks in his letters to his colleagues, such as Silas, Tychicus, Timothy and Titus, or about them would make a useful study for bishops similarly engaged in collaborative ministry. Paul is appreciative and supportive and yet at the same time encouraging and challenging. These texts show that God's grace comes to the Church through the messengers whom he sends as they work together – that is to say through persons chosen by God for this purpose. Divine wisdom is not available in its fullness to a single individual; it is distributed in such a way that individuals have to combine together to access it. Bishops are not like the Old Testament prophets, who often received divine inspiration in isolation and were forced to plough a lonely furrow. They are more like the apostles gathered in the upper room on the Day of Pentecost on whom the Spirit came collectively – and the apostles were not the only ones present (Acts 1.13–14; 2.1–4). The anointing comes and overflows when God's servants are united in solidarity (Psalm 133).

The *communal* dimension refers to the intimate relationship between the minister and the whole body of the faithful, because (as *BEM* puts it) 'the exercise of the ordained ministry is rooted in the life of the community and requires the community's effective participation in the discovery of God's will and the guidance of the Spirit'. This process of seeking to discern the Holy Spirit's guidance in a communal way takes place through various synodical structures and processes where the bishops have a particular, though not an exclusive responsibility for key areas of the Church's life and mission, namely doctrine, worship and ministry as a whole, hence the familiar Anglican expression, 'the bishop in synod'. A synod without the bishop or bishops is an incoherent idea; and a gathering of bishops alone is more than a synod: if it takes decisions or makes rulings, it is a council; if not, it is a conference (cf. the Lambeth Conference). A synod is the Church gathered in a representative way in the course of its journey – one could say, its missionary journey, borrowing a phrase from the labours of St Paul – because 'synod' means literally 'together on the way' (Greek: *sun hodos*). Synodality or conciliarity is an intrinsic dimension of the Church's life and has been so from the beginning (in the form of the Council of Jerusalem: Acts 15). It is part of the responsibility of bishops to preside at a synod (though this does not mean that the bishop should necessarily chair all the proceedings).

How does episcopal collaboration work in practice?

Of course, not everything can be shared. There are some burdens that a bishop has to shoulder alone. The bishop knows where the buck stops. There are confidences that bishops have to keep to themselves to their dying day and there are decisions that only they can take. A personal support group may help the bishop to carry the burden. A spiritual director may help to ensure that she/he carries it in a way that is conducive to his or her own spiritual life and walk with God. Collaborative ministry is not about pretending that absolutely everything can be shared or that all have equal responsibilities: it entails a division of labour to obtain maximum efficiency and effectiveness. This involves a kind of collegiality between bishops on the one hand and clergy and lay people on the other.

In many dioceses there will be a small, fairly tight-knit group around the bishop that is concerned with the oversight of ministry and mission in the diocese. It will probably consist of the diocesan bishop, any suffragan or assistant or coadjutor bishops, the archdeacons (if there are any), the dean of the cathedral, the diocesan secretary or chief executive and perhaps (at least for certain agenda items) the specialist heads of diocesan departments or programmes. The flourishing of the whole diocese will depend on the effectiveness of this meeting. If the meeting works well, the mission of the diocese will go forward, but if the meeting is dysfunctional, the diocese as a whole will suffer and struggle. So a good deal hangs on the model that the bishop and the bishop's closest colleagues adopt for their work together. This gathering is sometimes styled 'the bishop's staff', sometimes 'the bishop's team'.[5] The choice of nomenclature may well indicate a preference on the part of the bishop for one model over another.

The model of the bishop's staff goes back to the *familia* or household of the bishop in the early middle ages in Europe. The household's sole reason for existence was to enable the bishop to carry out his ministry effectively. The household provided practical support, prayer, secretarial assistance and informed advice when asked. This model is very hierarchical, if not feudal, and presupposes a strong form of monarchical episcopacy. It does not play well today, except perhaps in very traditional societies – but there the resources of support are unlikely to be available to a sufficient extent.

More acceptable, more workable, in a society that aspires to equality, mutual respect and participation in decision making is the team model. And this, it seems to me, fits with the New Testament metaphors of the body of Christ and servant ministry. Every member of the 'bishop's meeting', including the bishop him- or herself, is there to promote the well-being, the flourishing of the diocese as the community of word, sacrament and pastoral care that is called by God through the gospel and gathered around the bishop. In one sense, the meeting exists to support the bishop because the bishop is the chief pastor, principal minister of the sacraments, father (or mother) in God, ordinary and so on, of that diocesan community. But in another and overriding sense the meeting exists for the sake of the diocese, the people called by God in that particular place to love, worship and serve God and all persons. When all members of the bishop's team meeting (as we do well to call it) see it in that light, a sense of common purpose and mutual loyalty will be generated and good work will proceed from it. Of course, every team needs a team leader and this is unquestionably the role of the bishop. But the team also needs to be open-textured enough to allow entry to all needed sources of information, wisdom, insight and energy – and hierarchical, top-down ways of working are not conducive to opening the windows to that kind of imaginative rethinking.

There is a special relationship between the bishop and the presbyters in a diocese. Vatican II says of the bishop: 'His priests, who assume a part of his duties and concerns, and who are ceaselessly devoted to their work, should be the objects of his particular affection. He should

5. These ideas have been explored briefly in a private paper by Michael Sadgrove, at the time the Dean of Durham, England, in 'The role of the bishop's staff: Some provisional and personal reflections'.

regard them as sons and friends.'[6] Presbyters belong to their own college, though this is an underdeveloped idea, with little purchase in practice: much more could be made of the solidarity and fellowship between presbyters – provided that the college did not become a sort of trade union! The relationship between bishop and presbyters is not, strictly speaking, collegial – both presbyters and bishops have their own college – but it is collaborative. In the early Church, the bishop would sit, presiding at the celebration of the Eucharist, surrounded by his presbyters and assisted by his deacons.[7] The bishop was placed in the council of his presbyters to consult with them, to guide them and to pray with them. As John Halliburton wrote: 'If, therefore, the bishop in his person represents the faith and convictions of the local Church, then he is obviously bound to spend much of his time consulting with the whole body of Christians in his diocese in order to listen with them to what the Spirit is saying to that church.'[8] Like St Augustine, bishops will see themselves as 'fellow learners' with the people of God.

Since the bishop is also a priest (presbyter), there is a double bond of fellowship between the bishop and his or her priests. With them the bishop is a priest; for them she/he is a bishop. As we have seen, in 1 Peter 5.1–4 the Apostle Peter (or a writer speaking in his name) identifies himself with the presbyters/elders: 'Now as an elder (*presbuteros*) myself … I exhort the elders (*presbuteroi*) among you to tend the flock of God that is in your charge, exercising the oversight (*episkope*) … Do not lord it over those in your charge, but be examples to the flock.' In other words, the under-shepherds, whether bishops or presbyters, must work together harmoniously in the service of the 'Chief Shepherd'. Traditionally, there is also a special, even unique, bond between the bishop and the deacons, the deacons being part of the bishop's household in an extended sense.

So far this discussion of collegiality has been a purely clerical affair. But neither the bishop nor the priest will get very far unless they can find ways of working collaboratively with lay people too. Baptized into Jesus Christ's messianic identity, all the faithful share his anointing as Prophet, Priest and King. They fulfil their royal priesthood in their service to Kingdom and Church. The bishop's task, working with the

---

6. *Christus Dominus*, §16 (Flannery translation, pp. 572–573).

7. John Zizioulas, *Eucharist, Bishop, Church: The Unity of the Church in the Divine Eucharist and the Bishop during the First Three Centuries*, E. Theokritoff (trans.) (2nd edition, Brookline, MA: Holy Cross Orthodox Press, 2001).

8. John Halliburton, *The Authority of a Bishop* (London: SPCK, 1987), p. 26.

presbyters and deacons, is to enable them to fulfil their calling more fully and more perfectly, to the glory of God. In some Anglican Churches (the Church of England is one), churchwardens in every parish are the bishops' officers; though elected by parishioners, they are 'the eyes and ears of the bishop'. In other Anglican and Episcopal traditions, the local Vestry and its officers play a similar role. Churchwardens, Vestries and their equivalents are generally an under-rated and under-appreciated body of people who are called into a collaborative relationship with the bishop. In many Anglican Churches, there will also be a Bishop's Council, made up of other bishops (if any), clergy and lay people, whose role is to advise the bishop and to steer diocesan policy, including financial policy. Similarly, the diocesan synod is another opportunity for the bishop to work collaboratively with lay people and by this means to build each other up in their faith and ministry and extend the scope of Christ's Kingdom. By carrying out a collaborative ministry the bishop models it for the whole diocese and so enhances the fellowship or *koinonia* of the people of God committed to his or her care. At the same time a collaborative approach gets more work done more willingly and more effectively. It is a value-added method of working.

Chapter 6

THE BISHOP AND THE ANGLICAN COMMUNION

The ecclesiology of the Anglican Communion

Every bishop is, according to Anglican rites, ordained a bishop in the Church of God. With all the baptized we are placed, located, by the Holy Spirit at the heart of the one Church. What is required of all the faithful *vis-à-vis* the Church can be expressed simply but challengingly: to love God is to love God's Church and, in particular, that portion of it in which God has placed us. Bishops are known as lovers of God and of God's Church. It is easy to be in love with the ideal Church, the Church in the abstract, the Church that we will never have to cope with from day to day. But it is much harder to love the actual, concrete Church of which we are living members and which we come up against, with all its rough edges, every day. So the Anglican Communion will be very dear to all Anglican bishops. They will long for its well-being, its unity and its integrity, and will pray, study and work to those ends.

But what sort of body is the Anglican Communion? How should we describe and define it? We search in vain for exact comparisons.[1] Although we often hear the expression 'the Anglican Church worldwide'

---

1. Cf. Norman Doe, *An Anglican Covenant: Theological and Legal Considerations for a Global Debate* (London: Canterbury Press, 2008), pp. 47–51. For an analysis of recent developments in the Anglican Communion see Bruce Kaye, *Conflict and the Practice of Christian Faith: The Anglican Experiment* (Eugene, OR: Cascade Books; Cambridge: Lutterworth, 2011). Cf. also Ephraim Radner and Philip Turner, *The Fate of Communion: The Agony of Anglicanism and the Future of a Global Church* (Grand Rapids, MI: Eerdmans, 2006). In this section I have adapted some material from Paul Avis, 'Anglican Ecclesiology and the Anglican Covenant', *Journal of Anglican Studies*, 12.1 (2014), pp. 112–132.

or something similar, the Anglican Communion is clearly not a single, global church. Its organization is not that of a global church: it is much looser, more dispersed, somewhat disjointed. Worldwide Anglicanism lacks some of the attributes of a single church. There is no universal canon law of the Anglican Communion, no central legislative organ, no comprehensive oversight, no overall disciplinary framework and no common policy-making body.[2] Unlike the Roman Catholic Church, the Anglican Communion is not a global church.

But neither is the Anglican Communion simply a loose collection of churches, a mere ragbag of ecclesial bodies. That is to say, it is not simply a confederation of separate churches of diverse character that find it convenient to meet from time to time, in a pragmatic way, to consult and confer. The life of our Communion is different to that and stronger. Worldwide Anglicanism has a common ecclesiology. So it is not quite the same sort of animal as the Lutheran World Federation or the World Methodist Council, both of which contain churches with different ecclesiologies – in particular, episcopal and non-episcopal ecclesiologies. Within the Anglican Communion there is a shared fundamental ecclesiology, though there is some variation of polity from one church to another. That is to say, the theological principles of the member churches are held in common, though their practice of governance is not everywhere identical.[3]

The ecclesial configuration of the Anglican Communion is closest to that of the Eastern Orthodox Churches. The affinity between

2. There is, however, a substantial body of canonical principles that can be drawn from the corpus of the canons of the Churches of the Anglican Communion and which is held in common by those Churches: see *The Principles of Canon Law Common to the Churches of the Anglican Communion* (London: Anglican Communion Office, 2008): http://www.acclawnet.co.uk/canon-law.php

3. Cf. Colin J. Podmore, 'A Tale of Two Churches: The Ecclesiologies of the Episcopal Church and the Church of England Compared', *Ecclesiastical Law Journal*, 10 (2008), pp. 34–70; reprinted in *International Journal for the Study of the Christian Church*, 8 (2008), pp. 124–154. At least some of what Dr Podmore calls differences of ecclesiology, I would understand as differences of polity – though of course polity should always be grounded in ecclesiology and always has ecclesiological implications. Sometimes it is not easy to draw a clear line between ecclesiology and polity.

certain aspects of Anglican and Orthodox ecclesiology has often been noted.[4] Just like Orthodoxy, with its concept of autocephaly (each church with its own head) and its lack of a centralized organization, the Anglican Communion consists of self-governing churches that are in a relationship of communion with one another. As such, they consult and confer from time to time; they recognize a common bond and they seek to act as one wherever possible. Like Orthodoxy, Anglicanism is united by a shared faith, shared sacraments and a shared ministry focused in the episcopate. And, just like Orthodoxy, our experience of communion is sometimes damaged by disagreements about leadership, disputes about jurisdiction and even impairment of communion. However, the Anglican Communion has a more structured global common life than Orthodoxy has. Orthodoxy does not have the equivalent of all of our Instruments of Communion. Although the role of the Ecumenical Patriarch is comparable in some ways to that of the Archbishop of Canterbury, as *primus inter pares* among the bishops and metropolitans, there is no exact parallel in Orthodoxy to the other three Instruments of Communion: the Lambeth Conference, the Primates Meeting and the Anglican Consultative Council.

The Lambeth Conference is of particular importance to all Anglican bishops. From its first meeting in 1867, the Lambeth Conference of bishops has met approximately every ten years since. Convened and presided over by the Archbishop of Canterbury, the conference gathers in the Archbishop's diocese for prayer and worship, Bible study and theological reflection, the sharing of experience and mutual counsel, in order to offer guidance to the Communion and the world. While its statements have no legal authority until and unless they are accepted by the member churches through their own deliberative and legislative structures, they carry very considerable moral and pastoral authority as the guidance given by those – the chief pastors of the Church – who are

---

4. *Anglican-Orthodox Dialogue: The Dublin Agreed Statement 1984* (London: SPCK, 1985), §28, p. 18: '… even though the seniority ascribed to the Archbishop of Canterbury is not identical with that given to the Ecumenical Patriarch, the Anglican Communion has developed on the Orthodox rather than the Roman-Catholic pattern, as a fellowship of self-governing national or regional Churches.'

called to this role.[5] They are to be weighed seriously and should not be lightly disregarded.

Altogether, it seems that the Anglican Communion is unique; there is nothing quite like it in Christendom. It has consistently described itself as a Communion of Churches. The Lambeth Conference 1930 defined the Communion as 'a fellowship, within the one, holy, catholic and apostolic Church, of those duly constituted dioceses, provinces, or regional Churches in communion with the see of Canterbury'.[6]

The Anglican Communion is made up of churches. In the Communion, we often refer to the member churches as 'provinces' and there is some authority for that in our documents, including in the key definition of Lambeth 1930 that I have just mentioned. But, the term 'province' is ultimately inadequate to describe the member bodies of the Communion. Several national Anglican Churches consist of more than one 'province'. But perhaps more importantly, the semantics of 'province' are not entirely appropriate. The term 'province' can suggest that the member churches of the Communion are outposts of some central body, like branch offices that relate back to head office.

In the Anglican Communion there is no hierarchy of churches; there are no inner or outer circles; there is no head office. Each church is on the same level of importance as every other church. All are equally self-governing; there cannot be degrees of autonomy. Either you are responsible for your own affairs or you aren't. The truth that the member bodies of the Communion are churches underlines their responsibility for their own affairs, under God. But churches not only have a responsibility for their own life and mission: they have responsibilities towards the wider Church as well. No church is the whole Church; therefore, no church can be self-sufficient. No church lives to itself. A church that tries to live to itself alone cannot be a church. The churches of the Anglican Communion are connected, not by an overarching organization, not by any kind of universal jurisdiction, but

5. On the four Instruments of Communion see the report of the Inter-Anglican Standing Commission on Unity, Faith and Order (IASCUFO) to the Anglican Consultative Council, November 2012: http://www.anglicancommunion.org/communion/acc/meetings/acc15/downloads/IASCUFO%20Complete%20Report%20to%20ACC.pdf

6. Lambeth Conference 1930, 'Resolution 49', in Roger Coleman (ed.), *Resolutions of the Twelve Lambeth Conferences 1867–1988* (Toronto: Anglican Book Centre, 1992), pp. 83–84.

essentially by mutual commitment, expressed in part by consultation. As the Lambeth Conference 1930 puts it, the member bodies of the Communion 'are bound together not by a central legislative and executive authority but by mutual loyalty sustained by the common counsel of the bishops in conference'.[7]

Many churches of the Anglican Communion define themselves in relation to the Church Catholic or in relation to the wider Communion, or – very appropriately – both together. For example, the Anglican Church of Canada declares in the Statement of Principles within its Constitution that it is 'an integral portion of the one Body of Christ composed of Churches which [are] united under the One Divine Head and in the fellowship of the One Holy Catholic and Apostolic Church'. The Episcopal Church, echoing the Lambeth 1930 statement, defines itself as 'a constituent member of the Anglican Communion, a Fellowship within the One, Holy, Catholic, and Apostolic Church, of those duly constituted Dioceses, Provinces, and regional Churches in communion with the See of Canterbury, upholding and propagating the historic Faith and Order as set forth in the Book of Common Prayer'.[8] The Church of England affirms in the first of its Canons that it 'belongs to the true and apostolic Church of Christ', and in the Preface to the Declaration of Assent (Canon C 15) it affirms that 'the Church of England is part of the One, Holy, Catholic and Apostolic Church, worshipping the one true God, Father, Son and Holy Spirit'.

So to be a church is to be placed in relation to the Church universal, the Church that is the Mother of us all. Particular churches and the universal Church cannot exist without each other. They are mutually constitutive, holding each other in being simultaneously.[9] It is only in living relationship with the universal Church that we can know the reality of catholic faith and order within our own community. The Holy Spirit and all the means of grace that the Spirit employs are given to the Body of Christ, which is a Spirit-bearing Body. As we indwell the Body we share in the Spirit and the Spirit's gifts. Each local Eucharistic assembly, gathered by its bishop, receives the fullness of the Church only as long as it remains in communion with other local churches – and intentionally, with them all. When churches

7. Coleman (ed.), *Resolutions of the Lambeth Conferences*, p. 84.

8. Constitution of The Episcopal Church, Preamble.

9. Cf. Paul McPartlan, 'The Local Church and the Universal Church: Zizioulas and the Kasper-Ratzinger Debate', *International Journal for the Study of the Christian Church*, 4 (2004), pp. 21–33.

are in communion they partake of catholicity. Catholicity cannot be predicated of churches that have chosen isolation. A solitary church is no church.

Now we can ask again, What is the Anglican Communion? Certainly not a global church, but not a mere federation of completely separate churches either. In reality it is a communion of churches, no more and no less – and that is the beauty of it. The churches of the Anglican Communion subsist in a relationship of communion with each other. They are at the same time self-governing and inter-related. Anglican churches are called to walk the tightrope between autonomy and interdependence. But what does that imply in theology and practice?

By calling ourselves a communion we are intentionally positioning ourselves in relation to the key New Testament Greek word *koinonia*, which is translated in our English Bibles as 'communion', 'fellowship', 'sharing' or 'partnership'. *Koinonia* speaks of sharing together in something greater than ourselves.[10] As we have already noted, it is our fellowship with the Father and the Son and with each other (1 John 1.3). It is our sacramental communion in the body and blood of Christ (1 Corinthians 10.16). It is our solidarity with the apostolic community and its faith (Acts 2.42). It is our practical partnership in proclaiming the gospel (Philippians 1.5). *Koinonia* points to our joint participation in the life of grace, our lived unity with God the Holy Trinity and with all the baptized (2 Corinthians 13.13). Through faith and the sacraments, the Holy Spirit has made us ontologically one in the body of Christ. To be united with baptized believers in the body of Christ is to be united with Christ himself. *Koinonia* is at the same time mystical and practical; profoundly spiritual and down to earth.

When we map this theological reality of communion (*koinonia*) on to the actual relationships between churches, expressed in numerous ecumenical agreements, we see that communion involves three dimensions: recognition, commitment and participation. First, *recognition* of one another, on the basis of apostolic faith and order, as sister churches belonging to the one holy catholic and apostolic Church; secondly, mutual *commitment* to live and act together in

10. But see the critical examination of this interpretation of *koinonia* in Andrew T. Lincoln, 'Communion: Some Pauline Foundations', *Ecclesiology*, 5 (2009), pp. 135–160 and my Editorial in the same issue, 'A Challenge to Communion Ecclesiology', pp. 132–134.

fellowship and to do this through appropriate conciliar channels; and, thirdly, unrestricted mutual *participation* in the sacramental life of the Church, that is to say, a common baptism and a shared Eucharist celebrated by an interchangeable ordained ministry. These three dimensions of mutual recognition, mutual commitment and mutual participation are the key components of ecclesial communion. They are what we thankfully enjoy – albeit with some impairment at the present time – in the Anglican Communion.

To be in communion brings privileges and responsibilities. We are called to maintain communion and to build communion.[11] Our duty to the Body is to uphold and strengthen its communion. For us this is not a grim duty, but the overflowing of charity – *agape, caritas* – without which, as Archbishop Thomas Cranmer's Prayer Book says, 'all our doings are nothing worth'. Charity is 'the very bond of peace and of all virtues'. It is a supreme expression of charity when we do all we can to remain in communion with our fellow Christians, who themselves are in communion with God the Holy Trinity. It is our communion with God and with our brothers and sisters in Christ's Church that constitutes us as Christians. Communion in charity is our very lifeblood; without it, as the collect says, we are counted dead before God.[12]

One of the sources of the Collect for Quinquagesima from the Book of Common Prayer, 1662, from which I have been drawing, is Ephesians 4.1–3. It resonates strongly with 1 Corinthians 13 and is a benchmark biblical statement of communion in charity:

> I therefore, the prisoner in the Lord, beg you to lead a life worthy of the calling to which you have been called, with all humility and gentleness, with patience, bearing with one another in love, making every effort to maintain the unity of the Spirit in the bond of peace. There is one body and one Spirit, just as you were called to the one hope of your calling, one Lord, one faith, one baptism, one God and Father of all …'

11. The Eames Commission stressed that all concerned in disagreements over the ordination of women should endeavour to live in the highest degree of communion that is possible: *The Eames Commission: The Official Reports* (Toronto: Anglican Book Centre, 1994).

12. See further Paul Avis, *Reshaping Ecumenical Theology* (London and New York: T&T Clark, 2010), chapter 10.

In the Anglican Communion much play has been made of 'the bonds of affection' and these are the bonds that are often appealed to in times of tension.[13] In spite of our diversity, there is indeed much genuine affection shared between Anglicans from one member church to another, from one continent to another, I am happy to say. But is the expression 'bonds of affection' robust enough for our needs at the present time, when relationships are strained and in some cases severed? It is not affection but charity that can take the strain. It is charity that draws us together as Christians and as churches. Communion infused with charity is the key to Anglican unity.[14]

Separation and breaking communion

In recent years some groups have left their particular Anglican Church and some Anglican Churches have declared themselves to be out of communion with others, mainly over issues of theological liberalism and human sexuality. In this situation it is appropriate to ask: 'In what circumstances is it biblically and theologically justified for individuals and churches to break communion?' Any particular decisions will be wrestled with in the forum of conscience, but the New Testament is instructive in this connection. The church at Corinth was riddled with problems: it bore the marks of heresy, schism, exclusivism, anarchy and immorality. Corinth was an utterly dysfunctional church. Yet in his letters to the Corinthians Paul calls the Corinthian Christians 'saints' and treats them as a church. It does not enter his head that he should separate from them – that would presumably make their divisions worse. As for the Galatians, they had even embraced 'another gospel' (Galatians 1.6–7), yet Paul treats them as churches and the idea of breaking communion with them does not enter his thoughts.

13. For example, The Lambeth Commission on Communion, *The Windsor Report 2004* (London: Anglican Communion Office, 2004), Foreword by the Most Reverend Robin Eames, Archbishop of Armagh, Chairman, p. 11: 'The "bonds of affection", so often quoted as a precious attribute of Anglican Communion life …'

14. I have deliberately not discussed the Anglican Communion Covenant in this *Handbook of Episcopal Ministry*. But I have set out my views in Avis, 'Anglican Ecclesiology and the Anglican Covenant'.

But other New Testament case studies suggest that there are certain circumstances when separation is justified and required. These circumstances are found when the faith of the Incarnation ('Jesus Christ come in the flesh') is denied – but only then. As the First Epistle of John tells us, this is how we recognize the spirit of the antichrist (1 John 4.2–4). If we turn to our own Anglican tradition, we find that the classical Anglican divines, from Richard Hooker in the sixteenth century to Daniel Waterland in the eighteenth, held that separation from a church is required when we ourselves are forced to affirm teachings or actions that we believe to be wrong – in other words, when those teachings or actions are forced on us and made conditions of church communion. The sixteenth-century Reformers, on the Continent of Europe and in England, taught that Christians should not separate from their church as long as the means of salvation, the ministry of word and sacrament, remained. For them, the existence of causes of scandal in a church was not a sufficient justification.[15]

The bishop is both a guardian of the faith and a focus of unity. These two aspects of the bishop's calling may sometimes be in tension as the bishop feels pulled in one way by personal theological conviction and in another way by the demands of unity. But it seems to me that the bishop should bear witness to the truth of the faith as she/he sees it by teaching and synodical involvement, working for unity in truth. The context of a bishop's ministry is not only the local church (diocese) but also the universal Church, and this theological truth is intensified by modern electronic communications. A bishop cannot fulfil his or her apostolic ministry of gospel truth by electing to become a focus of disunity. And so we turn now to the relation between the bishop and the unity of the Church, Anglican and ecumenical.

---

15. See further Avis, *Reshaping Ecumenical Theology*, chapter 8, 'Building and Breaking Communion'.

Chapter 7

THE BISHOP AND CHRISTIAN UNITY

Ordained as a focus and agent of unity, the bishop is called to work and pray for the healing of divisions in the body of Christ.[1] Rowan Williams writes, 'The bishop's authority ... is an authority to unify.' But how is this difficult task to be accomplished? Williams explains that the bishop is entrusted with 'the task of referring all sides of a debate to the unifying [Paschal] symbol over whose ritual recollection he presides', that is to say the Eucharist.[2] It falls to the bishop to spearhead not only mission but unity, both in the diocese and in the wider Church. But because it is not always clear what sort of unity God wants for God's Church, we may say that the bishop will work and pray for such unity as will be for the glory of God, the well-being of God's Church and the effectiveness of God's mission in the world.

Behind this basic statement of intention lies the profound biblical conviction that to pray and work for the unity of the Church is an imperative that is laid upon us by the Holy Spirit – an imperative that honours God, reveals the true nature of Christ's Church and commends the Christian gospel to those who do not yet believe. So, in working for the healing of division, the bishop will be seeking *visible unity in a common mission*.

The Scriptures themselves forge an inseparable connection between unity and mission, mission and unity. The two are fused together in biblical theology.[3] We see this inseparable connection between mission

---

1. Material in the first part of this chapter is adapted from material that I drafted for the Anglican-Methodist International Commission for Unity and Mission (AMICUM): *Into All the World: Being and Becoming Apostolic Churches* (London: Anglican Consultative Council, 2014).

2. Rowan Williams, 'Authority and the Bishop in the Church', in Mark Santer (ed.), *Their Lord and Ours: Approaches to Authority, Community and the Unity of the Church* (London: SPCK, 1982), pp. 90–112, at p. 99.

3. Paul Avis, *Reshaping Ecumenical Theology* (London and New York: T&T Clark, 2010), chapter 10.

and unity in the fact that the two commandments that are explicitly given by Jesus Christ to his apostles in the Gospels are to proclaim the gospel in word and sacrament and so make disciples of all nations (*mission*, Matthew 28.16 ff.) and to love one another as he has loved them, so that it will be visible to all that they are his disciples (*unity*, John 13.34–35).

The inseparable biblical connection between mission and unity is made particularly clearly in the Fourth Gospel. In John 10 Jesus says:

> I am the good shepherd. The good shepherd lays down his life for the sheep … I know my own and my own know me, just as the Father knows me and I know the Father. And I lay down my life for the sheep. I have other sheep that do not belong to this fold. I must bring them also, and they will listen to my voice. So there will be one flock, one shepherd. (John 10.11, 14–16)

Here we see that Christ will sacrifice his life for his own, those who hear his voice and follow his call (v. 3). Between him and his flock there is an intimate bond of trust and devotion: they 'know' each other as the Father knows the Son and the Son knows the Father (v. 14–15). Besides those gathered around him in his earthly mission, there are those, already known to God, who are to become disciples in the future: 'other sheep that do not belong to this fold' (v. 16). The Good Shepherd will seek to gather them also and they will respond to his call as they recognize his voice. He wants to have all the sheep together in one flock, enclosed in one sheepfold: 'they shall become one flock'. This outcome is characterized above all by *singularity*. There is one gate (v. 2, 7, 9), one flock and one shepherd. It is for this united flock that he will lay down his life. He will die to gather the sheep into one. The purpose of his death will not be completely fulfilled until they are one flock. The Good Shepherd's mission is to unite his sheep – and following in his footsteps, in the 'imitation of Christ', his under-shepherds have *a mission to unite* also. But how?

There is no specific blueprint for the unity of the Church in the New Testament, but certain key characteristics may be discerned. We turn to another passage in John's Gospel that resonates in important ways with the ones that we have just looked at: Jesus' prayer at the end of the 'Farewell Discourses'. In John 17.20–23 Jesus prays to the Father for the unity of his disciples. Just as in John 10, they are described as his 'own'. His own are those whom the Father has given him, those whom he has sent into the world. And, just as in John 10 the Good Shepherd has a concern for his 'other sheep', so here Jesus prays for his 'future' disciples:

'not only on behalf of these, but also on behalf of those who will believe in me through their word, that they may all be one' (v. 20–21). So what sort of unity is Jesus praying for here?

The unity for which Jesus prays in John 17 is first of all a *spiritual*, or we may say a *mystical* unity. It is grounded in the mutual indwelling or 'abiding' of the Father and the Son and of believers with the Father and the Son and therefore exceeds our meagre grasp; it is unfathomable, a profound mystery. The unity or communion of Christians participates in that mutual abiding or indwelling that enfolds Father, Son and disciples in one and reflects it to the world. To abide in Christ is to abide in his word and in his love. In the Gospel of John, Christ's person, his words and his love are three ways of expressing the presence of Christ, three facets of the one Christological reality. But love is the key to all that Jesus speaks of here. The union of which this prayer speaks is a union of love, whether it is the mutual love of Father and Son, or the love that they bear towards humankind, or the love that disciples have for the Lord and for one another in return ('We love because he first loved us': 1 John 4.19). Christ's high-priestly prayer is then for a mystical work of God to take place that will unite God and God's people: 'I in them and you in me, that they may become completely one' (Greek: *teleioun*, 'may be perfected into one').

Here we see how the love that continually pours from the heart of God finds an embodiment in the communion of the Church. To seek to be and remain in communion with our fellow Christians is a fundamental expression of the love that we should have towards them. Love is shown in practice in many ways, but in the context of the Church love takes the form of communion. Communion is a form of grace. It cannot be achieved by our own efforts, it is not a human achievement, but at the same time it needs some structural supports to enable it to flourish. To do all we can to realize and maintain communion or unity is an expression of Christian love.

Secondly, the unity for which Jesus prays in John 17 is a *visible* unity, a unity such that it is apparent to all: 'that the world may believe that you have sent me'; 'so that the world may know that you have sent me and have loved them even as you have loved me' (v. 21, 23). When the Church remains in communion with the Father and the Son it manifests his glory to the world. It is a world-facing unity as well as a God-facing unity. The unity that God wants for the Church has its face turned towards the world. The unity that Christ desires for his Church must be unambiguously visible to the world in such a way as to convince the world of the truth of his mission (cf. John 16.8–11).

Thirdly, the unity for which Christ prays in John 17 is a *missional* unity. To have a mission is to be sent with a purpose. Both Jesus and his disciples are sent: 'As you have sent me into the world, so I have sent them into the world' (v. 18). This sentence is sandwiched between two statements that together speak of Jesus and the disciples being made holy in God's truth: 'Sanctify them in the truth; your word is truth ... for their sakes I sanctify myself, so that they also may be sanctified in truth' (v. 17, 19). In the Fourth Gospel it is said again and again that the purpose for which Jesus was sent and came into the world was to 'bear witness to the truth'. Before Pontius Pilate, Jesus solemnly states: 'For this I was born, and for this I came into the world, to testify to the truth.' And in an echo of the discourse on the Good Shepherd in John 10, he adds: 'Everyone who belongs to the truth listens to my voice' (John 18.37). The expression 'the truth' in John, as elsewhere in the New Testament, refers to God's revelation made known through Jesus Christ – in his coming, life, teaching, actions, death and resurrection. The incarnate one is 'full of grace and truth', for 'grace and truth came through Jesus Christ' (1.14, 18).[4] In the Fourth Gospel the unity for which Christ prayed will result in missionary outreach to the world, through giving open testimony to the truth of God's revelation and saving action in Jesus Christ.

Full visible unity

The goal of the ecumenical movement, and particularly of the Faith and Order movement within it, is and always has been, since the beginning of the twentieth century, the full visible unity of the Church of Jesus Christ. There is a solid ecumenical consensus regarding this aim. The impetus for this vision came originally from the mission field where the demand for a united witness and proclamation in the face of other faiths was irresistible. The Church's proclamation of the gospel is made not only in words, that is to say in preaching and teaching, vital though they are, but also through the celebration of the sacraments and the provision of pastoral care and oversight, expressed in many forms,

---

4. C. K. Barrett, *The Gospel According to St John: An Introduction with Commentary and Notes on the Greek Text* (London: SPCK, 1955), p. 426; C. H. Dodd, *The Interpretation of the Fourth Gospel* (Cambridge: Cambridge University Press, 1953), pp. 170–178.

including work for justice, peace and the integrity of God's creation. These are all aspects of the *total presence of the Church to the world*, its comprehensive communication of the gospel, because the Church's message is conveyed in both word and deed, in actions as well as speech. Those actions include its multifaceted pastoral ministry, a ministry of compassion, care and the healing of human identity in Christ. So questions of ministry and ordination, sacramental theology, pastoral authority and structures of oversight cannot be kept out of initiatives for a united witness.

The imperative of seeking a visibly united testimony to the world in evangelization has remained the guiding thread of the ecumenical movement, from its formal beginnings in the World Missionary Conference of 1910 in Edinburgh to the message of the Tenth Assembly of the World Council of Churches in Busan, South Korea, in 2013.[5] One of the foundational statements of this vision of visible unity was the 'Appeal to All Christian People' made by the 1920 Lambeth Conference of Anglican bishops from around the world. Addressing all baptized persons within the universal Church, the Appeal declared:

> We believe that God wills fellowship. By God's own act this fellowship was made in and through Jesus Christ, and its life is in his Spirit. We believe that it is God's purpose to manifest this fellowship, so far as this world is concerned, in an outward, visible and united society, holding one faith, having its own recognised officers, using God-given means of grace, and inspiring all its members to the world-wide service of the Kingdom of God. This is what we mean by the Catholic Church.[6]

The Appeal pointed out that this visibly united fellowship was not yet present in the world (i.e. the Roman Catholic Church was not it). The Church was divided: on the one hand were the ancient episcopal communions of East and West, the Orthodox and Roman Catholic Churches, to which (the Appeal noted) 'ours is bound by many ties

---

5. https://www.oikoumene.org/en/resources/documents/assembly/2013 -busan/adopted-documents-statements/message-of-the-wcc-10th-assembly

6. This and the following quotation from the *Appeal* are from M. Kinnamon and B. E. Cope (eds), *The Ecumenical Movement: An Anthology of Key Texts and Voices* (Geneva: World Council of Churches; Grand Rapids, MI: Eerdmans, 1997), pp. 81–83.

of faith and tradition'. On the other hand, there were the 'great non-episcopal Communions, standing for rich elements of truth, liberty and life which might otherwise have been obscured or neglected'. With these communions, the Lambeth bishops added, 'we are closely linked by many affinities'. Then we come to the heart of the Lambeth Appeal:

> The vision which rises before us is that of a Church, genuinely Catholic, loyal to all Truth, and gathering into its fellowship all 'who profess and call themselves Christians', within whose visible unity all the treasures of faith and order, bequeathed as a heritage by the past to the present, shall be possessed in common, and be made serviceable to the whole Body of Christ.

The Appeal went on to restate the 'Lambeth Quadrilateral' of 1888, which was derived from the 'Chicago Quadrilateral' of the (then) Protestant Episcopal Church of the USA two years earlier, and was itself shaped by the writings of William Reed Huntington. The 'Appeal to All Christian People' affirmed that the visible unity of the Church would involve the 'wholehearted acceptance' of four elements:

1. 'The Holy Scriptures ... as being the rule and ultimate standard of faith.'
2. The 'Nicene' (i.e. Nicene-Constantinopolitan) Creed as 'the sufficient statement of the Christian faith' and either it or the Apostles Creed as the baptismal confession.
3. 'The divinely instituted sacraments of Baptism and Holy Communion.'
4. 'A ministry acknowledged by every part of the Church as possessing not only the inward call of the Spirit, but also the commission of Christ and the authority of the whole body.'

Continuing in the same trajectory – and cutting a long story short – the Third Assembly of the World Council of Churches, meeting in New Delhi in 1961, articulated a vision of unity that has not been superseded in its authority or surpassed in its description:

> We believe that the unity which is both God's will and his gift to the Church is being made visible as all in each place who are baptised into Jesus Christ and confess him as Lord and Saviour are brought by the Holy Spirit into one fully committed fellowship, holding the one apostolic faith, preaching the one Gospel, breaking the one bread,

joining in common prayer, and having a corporate life reaching out
in witness and service to all and who at the same time are united with
the whole Christian fellowship in all places and all ages in such wise
that ministry and members are accepted by all, and that all can act
and speak together as occasion requires for the tasks to which God
calls his people.[7]

Thirty years later, in 1991, the Canberra Assembly of the World
Council of Churches also enumerated the marks of what it called 'full
communion'. These were

> the common confession of the apostolic faith; a common
> sacramental life entered by the one baptism and celebrated together
> in one eucharistic fellowship; a common life in which members and
> ministries are mutually recognised and reconciled; and a common
> mission witnessing to the gospel of God's grace to all people and
> serving the whole of creation.

The Canberra statement went on to say that the goal of full communion
would be realized when all the churches were able 'to recognise in one
another the one holy, catholic and apostolic church in its fullness'. It
further specified that full communion would be expressed on the local
and the universal levels of the Church through councils and synods.[8]

The Canberra statement immediately went on to address the crucial
question of diversity in unity. It stated that 'diversities which are rooted
in theological traditions, various cultural, ethnic or historical contexts
are integral to the nature of communion'. But it went on to point out
that there must be limits to diversity. Diversity would be illegitimate
if it made impossible the common confession of Jesus Christ as God
and Saviour, 'the same yesterday, today and forever' (cf. Hebrews 13.8)
and if it impeded the Church's confession, faithful to Scripture and the
apostolic preaching, of a salvation that embraced the whole of humanity
and from which no one was excluded. Within these limits, diversity

7. Report of the Section on Unity, Third Assembly of the World Council
of Churches, New Delhi, 1961; Kinnamon and Cope (eds), *The Ecumenical
Movement*, p. 88.

8. http://www.oikoumene.org/en/resources/documents/wcc-commissions/
faith-and-order-commission/i-unity-the-church-and-its-mission/the-unity
-of-the-church-gift-and-calling-the-canberra-statement?set_language=en

could exist in harmony, contributing to the richness and fullness of communion.[9]

So we may say that *diversity in harmony* should characterize the unity we seek. The post-modern, developed world is suspicious of institutions and finds uniformity unattractive. For Christians today a uniform, institutional form of unity is unpalatable, as well as unattainable. But the culture of post-modernity is characterized not only by diversity and difference (sometimes amounting to incoherence and fragmentation), but also by a longing for harmony – harmony with one's deepest self, harmony in one's closest relationships, harmony within society and harmony with the natural environment. Unity, expressed as a harmony of different voices, will commend the Christian witness to our world. Through all our disagreements, ultimate harmony is what we long for – singing the praise of God and testifying to God's grace with one accord.

Building on these classic texts, numerous ecumenical dialogues have looked for four components of unity, which are now part of a broad ecumenical consensus:

1. A common confession of the apostolic faith, grounded in Scripture and set forth in the historic creeds
2. A common baptism and a single Eucharist
3. A common, interchangeable ministry of word and sacrament
4. A common ministry of oversight[10]

Where these four elements are found, we have, in a particular situation, the essential components of full visible unity. They meet the criteria that were set out by the Lambeth Conference in 1920 and that have been articulated by the major statements of WCC Assemblies. These elements obviously do not add up to a blueprint for a united Church, but together they provide a sketch or portrait of what should characterize that unity. In that portrait these four elements must be present, but their concrete form will vary from one situation to another. What is vital is

---

9. http://www.oikoumene.org/en/resources/documents/wcc-commissions/faith-and-order-commission/i-unity-the-church-and-its-mission/the-unity-of-the-church-gift-and-calling-the-canberra-statement?set_language=en

10. For example, *An Anglican-Methodist Covenant* (Peterborough: Methodist Publishing House; London: Church House Publishing, 2001), §101–102.

that the texture of communion will show that the Church is visibly one in the sight of the world, even though communion will remain diverse in terms of the cultural expressions of belief, worship and various areas of practice.

Several features of the way that the four elements – creed, sacraments, ministry and oversight – are portrayed in the faith and order tradition, from Lambeth 1920 to Canberra 1991, are worth pointing out:

- The four elements of unity are patently visible, manifested in time and space; they are apparent to the world.
- The four marks of full visible unity do not imply any particular organizational or institutional structure; this may vary from church to church.
- The vision of full visible unity, guided by the four key components, is intended to make a rich diversity possible. There is no assumption of uniformity of worship or organization, quite the reverse. The distinctive identities of the uniting churches must be respected and preserved.
- 'Full visible unity' refers to the unity of the whole Church, not merely the part to which we belong. It is not appropriate to describe a relation of communion or 'full communion' between two churches as 'full visible unity'.
- The unity of the Church is both God's gift and our task: each church should take whatever practical steps it can, however modest, with its partner churches, towards the full visible unity of the Church of Christ.

The bishop as a sign and focus of unity

The Anglican tradition sees the ministry of the bishop as a sign and focus of the unity of Christ's Church. The report *Episcopal Ministry* emphasizes the role of the bishop as a 'sign and focus of unity and communion', not only in the diocese ('local church'), but in the wider Church:

> … through the office of a bishop, the Church is maintained and strengthened in unity in the service of God and its witness to the world. In the local church the bishop focuses and nurtures the unity of his people; in his sharing in the collegiality of bishops the local church is bound together with other local churches; and, through the

succession of bishops the local community is related to the Church through the ages.[11]

Episcopal Ministry goes on to argue that, because this is the case, 'the loss of a common episcopate, the resulting existence of parallel episcopates and divisively diverse forms of oversight ministries, diminishes the sign of unity and continuity. Parallel ministries of oversight reflect an imperfect, restricted, or impaired communion.'[12] The report points out the damaging effects of a divided episcopate:

> A divided ministry damages the catholicity of the church and limits eucharistic communion. A local church which is not related through a ministry of oversight to all other Christians through the world fails to reflect the catholic fullness of baptismal unity … A single fellowship, served by a reconciled ministry, enables the Church to interpret and hand on the one Gospel in all its fullness.[13]

This report faithfully reflects the classical Anglican approach to the role of the episcopate in the unity of the Church. This approach has its roots in the writings of Church Fathers such as St Ignatius of Antioch (especially his letters to the churches in Magnesia and Smyrna) and St Cyprian of Carthage (especially in *The Unity of the Catholic Church*) and found its most important twentieth-century expression in Archbishop Michael Ramsey's study *The Gospel and the Catholic Church*.[14] This tradition maintains that without the existence of a common episcopate, which is to say an episcopate that is held in common by all the churches concerned, the unity of the Church is radically undermined and its mission seriously impaired.

Because Anglican Churches hold this view of the bishop as a focus of unity, they have insisted in their ecumenical dialogues that the visible unity of the Church must include the episcopate. This point was made in the famous *Appeal to All Christian People* that was issued by the

---

11. *Episcopal Ministry* [the 'Cameron Report'] (London: Church House Publishing, 1990), p. 161.

12. *Episcopal Ministry*, p. 161.

13. *Episcopal Ministry*, p. 161.

14. A. M. Ramsey, *The Gospel and the Catholic Church* (1st edition, London: Longmans, Green and Co., 1936; 2nd edition, London: SPCK, 1990).

Lambeth Conference in 1920. The *Appeal* repeats the point made by the Lambeth Conference of 1888 that the visible unity of the Church will involve 'a ministry acknowledged by every part of the Church as possessing not only the inward call of the Spirit, but also the commission of Christ and the authority of the whole body'.

The Lambeth Conference *Appeal* then goes on to claim that 'the episcopate is the one means of providing such a ministry' and proceeds to outline how it understands the ministry of the bishop and how it evaluates the ministry of churches that are not episcopally ordered:

> It is not that we call in question for a moment the spiritual reality of the ministries of those Communions which do not possess the episcopate. On the contrary we thankfully acknowledge that these ministries have been manifestly blessed and owned by the Holy Spirit as effective means of grace. But we submit that considerations alike of history and of present experience justify the claim which we make on behalf of the episcopate. Moreover, we would urge that it is now and will prove to be in the future the best instrument for maintaining the unity and continuity of the Church.[15]

The *Appeal* immediately made it clear that it was not talking about an autocratic form of prelacy: 'But we greatly desire that the office of a bishop should be everywhere exercised in a representative and constitutional manner, and more truly express all that ought to be involved for the life of the Christian family in the title of Father-in-God.'[16]

Loyalty to this ecclesiology has meant that Anglican Churches have consistently said to their ecumenical partner churches that do not have bishops in historic succession that visible unity, including an interchangeable ordained ministry and shared oversight, requires episcopacy as one of its elements. The mutual recognition of those marks of the Church mentioned in Article VII of the *Augsburg Confession* and Article XIX of the *Thirty Nine Articles*, namely the authentic preaching of the word and the due celebration of the dominical sacraments, though vital, is not in itself sufficient for the establishment of visible unity between churches that are currently separated from one another.

15. Text in G. K. A. Bell, *Documents on Christian Unity 1920–1930* (Oxford: Oxford University Press, 1930), pp. 3–4.
16. Bell, *Documents on Christian Unity 1920–1930*, pp. 3–4.

It is important to note the fact that Anglican Churches hold that the visible unity of the Church requires not only that there should be bishops in the historic succession, but that these bishops should be in full sacramental communion with each other. This means that they recognize each other as bishops of the Church Catholic and each other's ministries as ministries performed by such a bishop. Anglicans hold this view because they see the bishop as the sign and focus both of diachronic and of synchronic unity – unity in time and space. That is to say, the role of bishops is not only to link the 'local' church of which the bishop is the 'chief pastor' with the Christian Church down the ages, but also to link it with the other local churches in the world today. The historical dimension of unity is expressed partly through the transmission of authority when a bishop is consecrated (but also through the continuity of the episcopal see and perhaps most importantly through the faithful transmission of the faith from one generation to another). The contemporary dimension of visible unity is also expressed when bishops in communion, from various sees and various churches, take part in the laying on of hands at the consecration of a new bishop – the Council of Nicaea in AD 325 laid down that at least three bishops should do so. This dual expression of visible unity obviously depends on the faithful being in sacramental communion with their bishops and the bishops being in sacramental communion with each other. It is only where such sacramental communion exists that it makes ecclesiological sense to talk about one visibly united church.

The bishop working for Christian unity

There are a number of practical, concrete steps that the bishop as ecumenist can take in order to build trust and confidence with his or her ecumenical partners as a basis for joint initiatives in mission and ministry:

- Build good working relationships with 'opposite numbers' in other churches within the area of the bishop's responsibility, extending courtesy and hospitality to them and engaging in joint Bible study, seasons of prayer and theological reflection and times of retreat, so modelling in practice constructive ecumenical relationships for the clergy in their own situations.

- Be aware of the content of relevant ecumenical agreements and agreed statements involving the Anglican Communion, such as those with the Roman Catholic Church, the Orthodox Churches, the Lutherans, Methodists and Baptists and of the work of the World Council of Churches through the Faith and Order Commission.
- Have a special concern for relations with churches with whom the whole Anglican Communion is 'in communion' (the Old Catholic Churches of the Union of Utrecht; the Mar Thoma Church of South India; the Philippine Independent Church) and those Lutheran churches with whom their own church is in communion through regional agreements (in chronological order: Porvoo for the British and Irish Anglican Churches, Called to Common Mission for The Episcopal Church and Waterloo for the Anglican Church of Canada).
- Be up to speed with church legislation (in some Anglican Churches, ecumenical canons) that governs what is and what is not permitted in terms of shared ministry and joint worship with churches with whom Anglicans are not yet in communion, and note any guidance issued by the Inter-Anglican Standing Commission on Unity, Faith and Order (IASCUFO) – and implement it energetically!
- Appoint a first-class ecumenical officer/adviser.
- Visibly support and promote the Week of Prayer for Christian Unity and make use of the resources for reflection and prayer that are jointly produced by the Faith and Order Commission of the WCC and the Vatican's Pontifical Council for Promoting Christian Unity.

Chapter 8

THE BISHOP AND THE HISTORIC EPISCOPATE

All bishops of the Anglican Communion, like Roman Catholic, Orthodox and some Lutheran bishops, are ordained within 'the historic episcopate' (the fourth point of the Chicago-Lambeth Quadrilateral, 1920 version). What does this mean and why do Anglicans think it is important? To answer that question, we need to start a bit further back, with the question of the visible unity of Christ's Church and the interchangeability of ordained ministers.

As we have already noted, it is generally agreed in the ecumenical movement that one of the marks of visible church unity is a single, interchangeable ordained ministry. Other essential criteria of unity, notably agreement in the apostolic faith, may well be met in certain cases, but until there is an interchangeable ordained ministry, full visible communion is not a reality. Communion between churches cannot exist without an interchangeable ordained ministry. Here is a useful definition of 'interchangeability':

> The expression 'interchangeability of ministries' usually refers to a situation in relations between churches whereby the ordained ministers of one church are eligible to be appointed to ministerial offices in the other without undergoing re-ordination. The ministerial orders or ordinations of each of the churches concerned are mutually recognised as meeting all the requirements of the other for its own ministry.[1]

1. *In the Spirit of the Covenant: Interim Report (2005) of the Joint Implementation Commission under the Covenant between the Methodist Church of Great Britain and the Church of England* (Peterborough: Methodist Publishing House, 2005), p. 90, §7.3.1.

But why is the interchangeability of ordained ministers so important? To answer this question we need to reflect for a moment on the place of the Eucharist in the worship and mission of the Church. The most eloquent expression of the unity of the Church is to be found in the celebration of the Eucharist or Holy Communion. The Second Vatican Council described the Eucharist as 'the source and summit' of the Christian life and of the Church's worship.[2] Most Anglicans would not wish to disagree with that statement. 'Holy Communion', the culmination of the Eucharistic celebration, is a communion with God the Holy Trinity and with the redeemed people of God in the Body of Christ. It is, therefore, the highest expression and the most intense realization on this earth of that communion with God and with one another that alone makes the Church the Church.

Because the Eucharist is supremely important, all churches are very particular about whom they allow to preside at the liturgy. In many, if not most, churches this role is reserved to presbyters and bishops. In Anglicanism (as in Roman Catholicism and Orthodoxy) deacons are not ordained to presidency at the Eucharist, but assist the bishop or priest in the celebration. Those (non-Anglican) churches that allow lay presidency at the Eucharist do so under strict conditions. All churches see Eucharistic presidency as one of the highest privileges and greatest responsibilities of the ordained ministry.

While it is an important truth that the Eucharist is celebrated by the whole community (there is no other 'celebrant' than the gathered community), the role of the president at the Eucharist is crucial. The minister who presides at the celebration of the Eucharist has the responsibility of oversight, to ensure that the celebration follows our Lord's institution and the teaching and rules of the Church. All ministry in the Church, whether lay or ordained, is the ministry of Christ in and through his Body. Ministry cannot be a matter of human effort or achievement; it must mean the risen, glorified Christ ministering to his people in word, sacrament and pastoral care. Ministry at the Eucharist is therefore a form of *the ministry of Christ*. The one who presides has a key role as an instrument of the ministry of Christ in and through his body: bringing God's word to God's people, officiating at the table that is the Lord's, leading the people in their sacrifice of praise and thanksgiving to the Father, through the Son, in the power of the Spirit.

---

2. *Lumen Gentium*, §11.

One of the most painful signs of lack of unity, of division, in the Christian Church is when the ministers of one church cannot preside at a celebration of the Eucharist in another church. But when mutual interchangeability of Eucharistic presidency is possible it is clear that a high degree of visible unity has been realized. Interchangeable Eucharistic presidency is, then, a touchstone of ecclesial communion.

Interchangeable Eucharistic presidency is also a precondition for *unity in oversight* which is the fourth of the widely received marks of full visible unity. The pastors of the churches preside both at the Eucharist and in the community. They are called (in John Wesley's phrase) to watch over the people in love. Presidency at the Eucharist and presidency in the community or pastoral oversight, *episkope*, cannot be divorced. Pastors cannot be fully united in oversight if they are not united at the Eucharist.

The link between the unity that is expressed in the Eucharist and the unity that is expressed in oversight is particularly clear when bishops ordain. The sacramental and the pastoral aspects of oversight come together in the act of ordaining. Ordination is an expression of the bishop's oversight, and a united ordination is an expression of united oversight. When ministers of more than one church ordain new ministers together, with the laying on of hands and prayer, they express a high degree of unity. Anglican churches allow only ministers of churches with whom their own church is 'in communion' – sister churches, one might say – to participate in ordinations.

Apostolic communion in time and space

The history of the Church is scarred by acts of separation for which no one side can be held solely responsible. The life of the Church is full of anomalies and scandals caused by disunity. The Church today presents a picture to the world of disorder, division and fragmentation that radically undermines the credibility of the gospel. This is far removed from the Lord's intention as portrayed in John 17; indeed, it is its antithesis, a counter-witness to the gospel. Surely we cannot rest content in a position so far removed from the will of God and for which we are accountable to God. Each and every church, to the extent that it is separated from the whole, experiences loss and lack of completeness. When we feel deeply bereft of sacramental communion with our fellow Christians, we are motivated to seek from God the unity that is God's will and gift. Ecumenical endeavour seeks to restore the wholeness of the Church's *apostolic communion*, according to the revealed will of God.

The apostolic communion is a communion that is, so to speak, incarnated in this world. Although it is not *of* this world, it has a real, material existence, extending through time and space. In principle, the apostolic communion extends back through the continuous history of the Church to the mission of the apostles; and in principle it extends throughout the world today, uniting churches in a universal fellowship that is one with 'the apostles' teaching and fellowship' (Acts 2.42). The apostolic communion thus has both diachronic and synchronic dimensions, historical depth and contemporary extent. We now consider the dimensions of time and space in relation to the historic episcopate.

The expression 'the historic episcopate'[3] refers to the formal intention of Anglican and other churches that there should be *visible historical continuity* between the Church of today and the Church of the apostles – a visible historical continuity that is particularly embodied in episcopal ministry from age to age – so that we may be able to say with some credibility that there is one Church and that it is the same Church now as it was then. The idea of the historic episcopate does not require that there should be an empirically traceable manual transmission of ordination, going back to the apostles, in every case: that cannot be verified. The emphasis is on the *formal intention* of a church not to make a new church and not to ordain ministers merely for its own church, but to preserve the visible historical continuity of the Church from the beginning, in the belief that the Lord Jesus Christ

3. See the essays in J. Robert Wright (ed.), *Quadrilateral at One Hundred: Essays on the Centenary of the Chicago-Lambeth Quadrilateral 1886/88–1986/88* (*Anglican Theological Review*, March 1988, Supplement Series, Number Ten; Cincinnati, OH: Forward Movement Publications; London and Oxford: Mowbray, 1988), especially J. Robert Wright, 'Heritage and Vision: The Chicago-Lambeth Quadrilateral', pp. 8–46, for the historical context and possible sources and antecedents. In addition to the various reports noted elsewhere in this *Handbook*, the following works stand out among the extensive Anglican writings on the historic episcopate: A. J. Mason, *The Church of England and Episcopacy* (Cambridge: Cambridge University Press, 1914); Kenneth E. Kirk (ed.), *The Apostolic Ministry: Essays on the History and Doctrine of Episcopacy* (London: Hodder and Stoughton, 1946); Kenneth M. Carey (ed.), *The Historic Episcopate in the Fullness of the Church* (Westminster: Dacre Press, 1954).

instituted and intended that an ordered community – a body of people with certain tasks and structures – should continue his mission until the end of the age (Matthew 28.16 ff).

But why do Anglicans hold that the sign of the historic episcopate is an essential element of full visible communion? Why do Anglicans, without exception, practise ordination within 'the historic episcopate' – by bishops only for the consecration of bishops, by bishops and priests (presbyters) for the ordination of priests and by bishops only for the ordination of deacons?

The first thing that is important to say is that the historic episcopate is not the only element in the constitution of the Church that Anglicans think is important – though our ecumenical partners in churches that are not so ordered sometimes receive that impression! Anglicans have made a number of agreements with churches that are not ordered in the historic episcopate. This shows that Anglicans do not believe that no church could exist without it. If we were to say that, we would run into difficulties not only with regard to our ecumenical agreements with partner churches, whose authenticity of word and sacrament we have acknowledged, but also with respect to parts of the early Church, when the structures of catholicity were in the process of emerging. The historic episcopate cannot be the *sine qua non* of the Church (without which there is no church). Why then do Anglicans think it is so important?

For Anglicans the historic episcopate is *a necessary though not sufficient condition for visible unity*. It is possible for the historic episcopate to be restored in churches that have temporarily lost it (as in certain of the Nordic and Baltic Lutheran Churches), or it can be received from one of the participating churches in a unity scheme (as in the case of the Church of South India and the Church of North India). But the fact remains that Anglican Churches make agreements for ecclesial communion only with churches that are ordered in the historic episcopate or will become so ordered through that agreement, even if some loose ends and anomalies remain for a while. In maintaining this discipline Anglican churches believe that they are being faithful to the pattern of the early Church. They hold that this pattern comes down to the Church of today from apostolic or early post-apostolic times and that it carries the authority of the early tradition and also significant ecumenical support and consensus (as we see in *Baptism, Eucharist and Ministry*). Anglicans are also mindful that they have agreed statements with the Roman Catholic Church and the Orthodox Churches to which agreement on the historic episcopate is integral.[4] Moreover, Anglicans believe that the historic episcopate is 'the one means of providing ... a ministry acknowledged by every part of the Church as possessing not only the inward call of the Spirit, but also the commission of Christ and the authority of the whole body'.[5] It is worth reiterating that the *Appeal* immediately went on to affirm the 'spiritual reality' of the ministries of those Christian communions that did not have the historic episcopate. In affirming the place of the historic episcopate in our own churches and requiring it for full visible communion with other churches, we are following what we believe to be right and do not intend to pass any kind of judgement on churches that are not ordered in the historic episcopate.

Three key aspects of the historic episcopate stand out. First, it is *personal*. The historic episcopate refers to persons who have been entrusted with the responsibility of *episkope*, oversight. The responsibility of oversight may well be exercised by a corporate body, such as a synod (of which the bishops are part; hence the expression 'bishop in synod'), but that is not the same as the historic episcopate as such, which is necessarily vested in persons (who have been traditionally described as fathers in God). God did not send a committee to redeem the world, but a Person. As every Christian church recognizes, there is no substitute for personal pastoral ministry – with all its risks and vulnerability.

Second, the historic episcopate is *historic*: it is an expression of the visible historical continuity of the Church today with the Church of the apostles. It is one of the links – together with the Scriptures, the apostolic faith and the sacraments – that bind us to the Church of the New Testament. The historic episcopate is not dependent on an unbroken chain of hands on heads – though succession of ordinations is an important outward sign. It refers primarily to a church's *intention to ordain to the same ministry as that of the apostles within the same Church.*

Third, the historic episcopate is *received*. All the gifts and graces of the Christian life are received from God through God's Church. 'What do you have that you did not receive?', asks St Paul in 1 Corinthians 4.7. All our churches are debtors to the wider Church, the Church Catholic, and our highest aspiration is simply 'to do what the Church does' – not

4. Anglican–Roman Catholic International Commission (ARCIC), *The Final Report* (London: CTS/SPCK, 1982), especially 'Ministry and Ordination' (1973) and its 'Elucidation'; International Commission for Anglican-Orthodox Theological Dialogue, *The Church of the Triune God (The Cyprus Agreed Statement)* (London: Anglican Consultative Council, 2006).

5. Lambeth Conference 1920, *Appeal to All Christian People* (Resolution 9).

'our own thing'. I repeat that Anglicans have never said that a church cannot be a church without it – several ecumenical agreements made by Anglicans clearly show the reverse of that – but we believe that the historic episcopate is a precious aspect of catholicity, that is to say of the fullness and wholeness of the Church, the Church that was before we were and will endure after we are gone.

Bishops in communion

When bishops from churches in communion with each other come together to consecrate a new bishop an important sign of communion in time and space can be seen. This act both expresses and strengthens the visible unity of the Church and does so for several reasons.

Communion in time. The portion of the people of God entrusted to the pastoral care of the bishop is usually one that was in existence before the bishop arrived on the scene and one that will continue after the bishop has gone. The location of the bishop's ministry (the bishop's 'See') endures in time. The aspect of continuity is particularly evident in churches that have historic sees, many going back to the time when the Christian faith was first brought to that land (to mention just some of the most ancient: Canterbury in England, St David's in Wales and Armagh in Ireland). For the early Church, the continuity of the bishops in a see was a significant expression of the continuity of the Church and of its apostolic faith. Because bishops represent the churches they serve, their ministry speaks of the Church's continuity in time.

Communion in space. Collectively, bishops link together the churches that they lead. Bishops help to bring to visible expression the communion between their churches, holding them together in unity in the spatial dimension. The coming together of bishops to consecrate a new member of the episcopate in the Church of God is a signal witness to the unity of the Church and serves to cement that unity.

To those two dimensions – time and space – we can add two others.

Communion in faith. Bishops are entrusted at their consecration or ordination with the stewardship of the faith and are charged with safeguarding the teaching of the Church. They do this through their own teaching ministry and their oversight of the teaching ministry of others. The coming together of bishops to consecrate a new bishop expresses solidarity in the confession of the true faith. When bishops from churches that are in communion with one another join together in consecrating a new bishop they witness to the acceptability of the doctrine of that church and its bishop – there is a unity of confession. In this way, bishops in communion are seen as guardians of Christian doctrine.

Communion in authority. Finally, at such a *consecration in communion*, the bishop who is being ordained receives the authority to ordain other ministers. In this way the Church's ministry is reproducing itself. Ministers are ordained, not into their particular Anglican church, but into the universal Church of God. A consecration in communion is a witness against the fragmentation of the Church. By their action the bishops involved confess that there is one Church and one ministry. The participation of ordaining ministers from sister churches is an endorsement that the new minister is being ordained into the universal Church.

In all these ways, in the act of ordination a bishop is setting forward both the mission and unity of the Church.

Historic episcopacy and diocesan boundaries

Episcopal intervention[6] from one diocese to another is one of the difficulties that *The Windsor Report* attempted to deal with. In one of its 'moratoria', it urged that this practice should stop. Here the report was in line with the teaching of the early Church and in particular with the decrees of the Council of Nicaea, the first ecumenical council after the Council of Jerusalem mentioned in Acts 15. In AD 325, in its canon 6, Nicaea established two principles that govern the relation of local (i.e. diocesan) churches to each other: (1) the principle of the geographical division of the Church and the territorial integrity of church boundaries; and (2) the principle of obedience to higher authority and of subsidiarity in the Church on the basis of the historic episcopacy. The first of these principles (the integrity of diocesan boundaries) was established in the first part of Canon 6:

> Let the ancient custom which is followed in Egypt and Libya and the Pentapolis remain in force, by which the Bishop of Alexandria has the supervision of all those places, since this is also the custom of the Bishop of Rome. Similarly, in regard to Antioch and the other provinces, let the inherited rights of the churches be preserved.

The second of these principles (obedience to authority) was established in the second part of Canon 6: 'Certainly it is quite clear that if someone

6. This section is based on advice kindly provided by the Revd Canon Professor J. Robert Wright of The Episcopal Church.

has been made bishop without the consent of the metropolitan, this great council defines that such a one is not a bishop.' ('Metropolitan' here has become, in later Anglican terminology, a virtual equivalent to 'Archbishop' or 'Presiding Bishop'.)

This principle was endorsed at the time of the English Reformation by John Jewel, Bishop of Salisbury, who in his *Apology of the Church of England*, published in 1562, appealed to the sixth Canon of Nicaea to show that the Bishop of Rome had no more jurisdiction over the Church of God than other patriarchs.[7] Earlier, King Henry VIII, in the Ten Articles of 1536, had declared that the English Church repudiated any opinions that were condemned by any of the first four ecumenical councils, which obviously includes Nicaea. And Archbishop Thomas Cranmer, in his *Reformation of Ecclesiastical Laws* (1553/71), stated that 'we embrace and accept with great reverence' the decisions of the first four ecumenical councils, though they are to be tested by Scripture.[8]

In more recent times, these hierarchical and territorial principles of historic episcopacy were affirmed for Anglicans in resolution 11 of the third Lambeth Conference of Anglican Bishops in 1888, and again in resolution 72 of the Lambeth Conference of 1988, which affirmed worldwide Anglican 'unity in the historical position of respect for diocesan boundaries and the authority of bishops within these boundaries', stating that 'it is deemed inappropriate behaviour for any bishop or priest of this Communion to exercise episcopal or pastoral ministry within another diocese without first obtaining the permission and invitation of the ecclesial authority thereof.' This principle was reaffirmed in Lambeth 1998, Resolution V.13.

Thus the principle that bishops should respect the boundaries of the dioceses of their fellow bishops, even if they disagree strongly with those bishops' words or actions, just as they would expect other bishops to respect the integrity of their own see, has been affirmed by the first ecumenical council, the Anglican Reformers and the Lambeth Conference. Unilateral intervention is not the answer to disagreements in the Church; it usually makes them worse.

7. John Jewel, *An Apology of the Church of England*, ed. J. E. Booty (Ithaca, NY: Cornell University Press for the Folger Shakespeare Library, 1963).
8. Thomas Cranmer, *Reformatio Legum Ecclesiasticarum*, §1.4, in Gerald Bray (ed.), *Tudor Church Reform: The Henrician Canons of 1535 and the Reformatio Legum Ecclesiasticarum* (Woodbridge, Suffolk: The Boydell Press/ The Church of England Record Society, 2000), p. 183.

Chapter 9

THE BISHOP AS SCHOLAR AND THEOLOGIAN

A bishop is ordained to be a teacher and guardian of the faith. Therefore, every bishop is called to be a student of the Scriptures and of Christian theology. But is this realistic? A bishop's life is, for much of the time, a treadmill of ceaseless activity. There are calls upon the bishop's time and attention coming from left, right and centre – and not just in terms of ecclesiastical politics! For a bishop to study means carving out time for reading in a busy schedule. Michael Ramsey, Archbishop of Canterbury, said that he would resort with longing, in his spare moments, to his theological books, like a secret drinker returning to the bottle. Ramsey recommended a 'fourth Sunday rule': he aimed to keep one Sunday in four free from engagements because something would probably crop up, needing his attention, but if not, he would spend the day quietly at home among his books, recharging his batteries, and be a better preacher, as a result, on the other Sundays. John Habgood, Archbishop of York, would have his head in a book before his car had left the house (though that depends on having a driver, which often is not the case in the Anglican Communion). Ramsey and Habgood used every minute to snatch some reading. Some bishops, like some of their clergy, will make a rule to try to read at least one theological book each month and subscribe to a couple of journals, as well as church papers.

Bishops are expected to have something to say on all occasions. As well as the liturgical sermon, the talk to gathered clergy, or the set-piece presidential address at a diocesan synod, there are those times when the host says, 'Bishop, will you say a few words, please.' At such moments the words, 'I'd like to thank you all for what you do for the Lord,' are welcome, though predictable, but not nearly enough!

'Out of the abundance of the heart the mouth speaks' (Matthew 12.34). If there is little in heart and head, the words will be empty platitudes. They will not convey faith, hope, wisdom and encouragement to the hearers. The bishop needs a well-stocked mind, constantly refreshed and the ability to mull over what she/he has read and to select apposite thoughts. 'Every scribe who has been trained for the kingdom of heaven is like the master of a household who brings out of his treasure what is new and what is old' (Matthew 13.52). Not everyone can be Rowan Williams who, to our constant amazement, never failed to pull an unpremeditated but edifying rabbit out of the hat (mitre) on every conceivable occasion. But we can all leave our hearers with what St Paul calls a word of wisdom or a word of knowledge that builds up the church (1 Corinthians 12.8, 26).

Church papers and theological journals

The church papers vary from one part of the world to another, though electronic communication means that we can access our paper of choice almost wherever we are. Church papers are still quite politicized, so I am not going to suggest any particular ones – merely mentioning those best known to me because I contribute to them from time to time: the *Church Times* (Church of England), *The Tablet* (Roman Catholic, but read by many Anglicans) and *The Living Church* (The Episcopal Church). Some clergy and bishops claim to treat the church press with something approaching contempt, certainly with disdain, but I find that I usually learn something useful by spending twenty to thirty minutes with each of them.

Journals are a different matter, especially if they are peer-reviewed, which ensures a certain amount of objectivity. Here are some that I know well and would recommend:

Theology (edited by Robin Gill and published by SPCK) is usually
  stimulating and relevant to practice, with short pithy articles
  and lots of reviews to keep us up to date with current thinking,
  including in biblical studies.
Anglican Theological Review (edited by Ellen K. Wondra) is important
  for keeping up with the enormous amount of sound scholarship
  and creative reflection within The Episcopal Church.
Journal of Anglican Studies, formerly edited by Bruce Kaye and now
  by Andrew McGowan and published by Cambridge University
  Press, is currently attempting to broaden its range and to be
  more representative of the Anglican Communion; it deserves to
  be supported.

Ecclesiastical Law Journal (formerly edited by Mark Hill, now by Will Adam and published by Cambridge University Press) is essential reading for keeping up with the legal dimension of the bishop's ministry and interpreting changes in the juridical culture in which the Church operates – the international character of this culture being reflected in the coverage of the journal.

Finally, I will mention *Ecclesiology* in which I have an interest as the founder and editor-in-chief, along with an international and ecumenical team of editors and advisers. This journal is published by Brill and focuses mainly on mission, ministry and unity issues. It is a scholarly journal that aims to be useful to practitioners: www.brill.nl/ecso

Bible study

As well as books to foster theological reflection, a bishop needs to be nourished by the word of God and to be able to open the Scriptures and expound them in a way that has scholarly integrity. A bishop should be enthralled by the Scriptures, as should every priest and deacon – they are committed in their ordination to studying them. A bishop should not be put to shame by clergy and laity who are better versed in Bible study. That means doing some homework with reliable commentaries, especially on the books of the New Testament, and the ability to refer to the original Greek. Such preparation will not be paraded; the exposition that the bishop gives will be merely the tip of the iceberg of his or her understanding, but it will carry authority because of that fact. Basic information about biblical books and themes, and books about them, is of course freely available on the internet. Recommended reference works include the *Oxford Dictionary of the Christian Church* (3rd edition, Oxford University Press, 1997), the SCM series of Dictionaries and the *New Dictionary of Christian Ethics and Pastoral Theology* (IVP, 1995).

Here are some good Bible commentary series in English:

Black's New Testament Commentaries, published by Continuum/ Bloomsbury/Hendrickson and edited by Morna D. Hooker. One of the most recent in this series of manageable-sized, accessible commentaries is Andrew T. Lincoln, *The Gospel According to St John* (2005).
The New International Greek Testament Commentary, published by Eerdmans/Paternoster and edited by I. Howard Marshall and

Donald Hagner. Recent volumes include Anthony C. Thiselton, *The First Epistle to the Corinthians* (2000) and R. T. France, *The Gospel of Mark* (2002). These are hefty tomes and obviously require some knowledge of Greek.

International Critical Commentary, published by Bloomsbury T&T Clark. Though immensely detailed and requiring some knowledge of New Testament Greek, these volumes tend to be rich in suggestive reflection. The jewel in the crown is probably the three volumes on Matthew by W. D. Davies and D. C. Allison (1988–).

Word Biblical Commentary (New Testament editor Ralph P. Martin). The series on the Greek text of the New Testament dates from the 1980s, but retains much value. It contains, for example, James D. G. Dunn's two volumes on Romans.

SCM Theological Commentary on the Bible, published by SCM and Brazos. These are intended to be stimulating theological reflections on and applications of the Scriptures, rather than detailed exegesis of each verse. A recent volume is Stanley Hauerwas on Matthew (2006).

A sense of the Church

As chief pastors in the Church of God bishops live with a sense of the Church through history and in all its diversity. Our sense of the Church needs to be fed and nurtured. A hefty introductory volume on the Church is Gerard Mannion and Lewis S. Mudge (eds), *The Routledge Companion to the Christian Church* (Routledge, 2008). The *Oxford Handbook of Ecclesiology* (which I am editing) provides comprehensive resources for understanding the Church in Scripture, history and contemporary theology (Oxford University Press, 2016). A short guide to Anglican ecclesiology is my *The Anglican Understanding of the Church: A Introduction* (2nd edition, SPCK, 2013). A little more depth is provided in my *The Identity of Anglicanism: Essentials of Anglican Ecclesiology* (T&T Clark, 2008).

Nourishing the imagination

However, theological and biblical studies alone are not enough to nourish the heart, mind and spirit. We need to refresh the springs of imagination and to nurture creative reflection in order to keep insight alive. For this we turn to imaginative literature – the novel beside the bed and for whiling away long journeys by plane; poetry perhaps for the time of daily meditation and to take on retreat; biographies and autobiographies of Christian saints and leaders and of the great men and women of history always on the go. Reading ground-breaking work in other relevant disciplines – and a good many bishops have either a background or an interest in one of the physical or social sciences – is admirable, provided we are not tempted to regale our hearers with the latest raw, untested theories in our sermons and addresses. Altogether, intellectual, emotional and spiritual enrichment is not a luxury but a necessity and a priority.

The bishop as theologian

If theology is 'discoursing of the things of God', the *logos* of *theos*, then every thoughtful Christian is a theologian.[1] Our baptism, with its profession of the Trinitarian faith, mandates us to know and bear witness to the truth of God revealed in Jesus Christ. Every Christian has a 'homing instinct' (*sensus fidei*) for 'the truth as it is in Jesus'. However, to engage actively in theology as a calling goes well beyond the intuitive reflection of the believer. To do theology is to reflect in a disciplined, informed and critical way on the knowledge of God.

Many lay Christians, without an academic training, aspire to do this and some distinguished theologians have been or are lay people. However, all the Church's ordained ministers undergo a training that is intended to equip them for disciplined, informed and critical reflection on the faith of the Church. The calling to engage in theological reflection applies pre-eminently to those called to the episcopate. The Ordinal attached to the Book of Common Prayer, 1662, urges the episcopal candidate: 'Give heed unto reading, exhortation and doctrine. Think upon the things contained in this book [the Bible]. Be diligent in them.' At the ordination of a bishop in the Anglican Church of Canada the candidate is asked, 'Will you be faithful in prayer, and in the study of holy scripture, that you may have the mind of Christ?' In the Church of England the candidate is asked, 'Will

1. Some material under this heading is drawn from my chapter of the same title in T. W. Bartel, *Comparative Theology: Essays for Keith Ward* (London: SPCK, 2003), pp. 164–176. The material began life as a presentation at the College for Bishops when it was located at the General Theological Seminary, New York City, in the early 1990s.

you be diligent in prayer, in reading Holy Scripture, and in all studies that will deepen your faith and fit you to bear witness to the truth of the Gospel?' A bishop is charged, at his or her ordination and consecration, to study the Scriptures assiduously – to study them in the light of relevant learning and to interpret them in such a way as to refute error and to enlighten the faithful with the truth of God. The bishop is mandated not simply to proclaim, but also to interpret the Gospel. A bishop is required to be a theological interpreter, and to be a theological interpreter is to be both a student and a maker of theology.

The relationship between episcopal ministry and theological responsibility raises such questions as: Who has the authority to speak for the churches? What is the relationship between theological research and official teaching? Who sets the vision for the Church: bishops or theologians?[2] The lines of theologian and bishop – originally distinct in the early Church – had converged by the fourth century into the figure of the scholar-bishop, whose supreme exemplar is St Augustine of Hippo. A millennium later, the problems of the late medieval Western Church (the fragmentation of the papacy, the demand for the reform of abuses and the need to deal with 'heresies') required the contribution of conciliar thinkers. Three hundred scholars were present and voted at the great Council of Constance in 1514. The sixteenth-century Reformers were almost all pastor-theologians. Martin Luther, John Calvin, Thomas Cranmer and Martin Bucer united in themselves the calling to govern the church and the calling to be creative theologians. The Protestant tradition of scholarly leadership fed, three centuries later, into the early ecumenical movement. At the first assembly of the World Council of Churches in Amsterdam in 1948, one delegate commented that he saw before him practically all of the authors of the modern books on his shelves.

In some Protestant churches (e.g. the Evangelische Kirche in Deutschland [EKD]) it is the theologians, rather than the bishops, who have effective oversight of doctrine. The modern Roman Catholic Church has absorbed virtually all theological authority into the papacy, which under John Paul II and Benedict XVI rode roughshod over theological advisers and conferences of bishops alike. The theological renaissance that both heralded and flowed from the Second Vatican Council (1962–65) was effectively stifled. In 1969 a theological declaration signed by 1,360 Roman Catholic scholars in fifty-three countries rejoiced in the restoration of theological liberty by Vatican II. They were soon to be

2. Cf. W. A. Visser't Hooft, *Teachers and the Teaching Authorities: The Magistri and the Magisterium* (Geneva: World Council of Churches, 2000).

disillusioned. Over the past forty years, virtually all of the most creative Roman Catholic theologians have come into conflict with the Vatican authorities and many have been formally disciplined.

Where is Anglicanism in this debate about the oversight of doctrine? The most seminal of all Anglican theologians, Richard Hooker, was not a bishop, though both of his patrons, John Jewel and John Whitgift, were notable scholar-bishops, the latter Archbishop of Canterbury. The history of the Church of England shows a line of episcopal divines that, if not yet quite extinct, is now very tenuous.[3] In this respect, Anglicanism stands between Protestantism and Roman Catholicism. Unlike most Protestant churches, Anglicanism is episcopal in its ecclesial constitution, preserving the visible continuity of episcopal ministry through the 'historic episcopate' and, in the older Anglican provinces, in Britain and Ireland, through the succession of bishops in historic sees. But, unlike the Roman Catholic Church, Anglicanism is not particularly hierarchical. There is a striking difference between the Roman Catholic notion of the 'hierarchical communion' of bishops with each other and with the Pope, who is the head of the episcopal college and without whom it cannot act and in fact has a rather shadowy existence, and the Anglican understanding of episcopal collegiality, even granted the modest, though real, place given to primacy in Anglican polity.[4] For this reason Anglicanism may be well placed to distinguish the teaching ministry of the bishop from the role of theological exploration and creativity. Every bishop is called to be a guardian and teacher of the faith by virtue of their office. But the formal articulation of doctrine is usually the responsibility of synods, where laity and clergy, as well as bishops, have the task of discernment.

In some cases deep theological exploration by a bishop may require greater freedom than the office can sustain. An episode from the recent past is instructive here. In the 1980s The Church of England was shaken

3. For Hooker and a galaxy of scholar-bishops through the centuries, see Paul Avis, *Anglicanism and the Christian Church* (revised edition, London and New York: T&T Clark, 2002) and Paul Avis, *In Search of Authority: Anglican Theological Method from the Reformation to the Enlightenment* (London and New York: Bloomsbury T&T Clark, 2014). See also G. K. A. Bell, 'The Church and the Theologian', in G. K. A. Bell and A. Deissmann (eds), *Mysterium Christi: Christological Studies by British and German Theologians* (1st edition, London: Longmans, 1930), pp. 277–84.

4. Vatican II, *Lumen Gentium*, §22; Podmore, *Aspects of Anglican Identity* (London: Church House Publishing, 2005).

by the so-called Durham affair. David Jenkins, formerly a teacher of theology in the University of Oxford and professor of theology at the University of Leeds, but by then the Bishop of Durham, the fourth most senior bishopric in the Church of England after Canterbury, York and London, publicly questioned the literal interpretation of two credal tenets: the virginal conception of Jesus and his physical resurrection. Half of the nation became intensely agitated by the spectacle of a senior bishop seeming to undermine the faith. Excitement mingled with indignation as the finer points of theology were discussed wherever two or three were gathered together throughout the land, especially in the local pub. Jenkins had touched a nerve in the half-Christian psyche of the nation. On the one hand, he seemed to articulate the questions of honest doubters, to air what many had been thinking privately. On the other hand, he seemed to be betraying his calling as a bishop, a guardian of the faith. The ambivalence of his position was clear to millions who were not regular churchgoers. In the more reflective discussions attention was focused on the role of a bishop. Is it compatible with being an academic scholar? Is it right for a bishop to question traditional beliefs? Does theological exploration always lead to doubt? The Durham affair led directly to the report of the House of Bishops of the Church of England on *The Nature of Christian Belief* in 1986 and indirectly to the report of a group set up by the two English Archbishops on *Episcopal Ministry* (1990).

Episcopal Ministry gave due weight to the bishop's role as teacher and guardian of the faith, but said little about the bishop as theologian. In contrast, a statement on 'The Ministry of Bishops', issued by the House of Bishops of The Episcopal Church of the USA in 1991, emphasized a much more creative role for the bishop: 'to transmit the tradition ... is to interpret it: to grasp new dimensions of its meaning, to envisage it in fresh perspectives'.[5]

Episcopal Ministry set out a rather daunting ideal of a bishop:

[O]ur bishops should be strong teachers of the faith who are both deeply engaged in the continuing education of the people of God ... and powerful defenders of the faith and winners of souls in the world ... There must be well-balanced expository preaching of

5. J. Robert Wright (ed.), *On Being a Bishop: Papers on Episcopacy from the Moscow Consultation 1992* (New York: The Church Hymnal Corporation, 1993), p. 90 (para. 16).

the Scriptures... sensitive and hopeful response to the challenge of our society, and to human need in our time... a steady endeavour to fill minds and souls with the greatness of a vision that looks to an eternal future.

The report added that the bishop enjoys 'rich opportunities of speaking and writing, in the media as well as directly to his people, on matters of both faith and morals; and of reaching in this way those who have not as yet had a real opportunity of hearing the Gospel' (p. 288). Teacher, preacher, apologist, defender of the faith, evangelist, inspirer, visionary, prophet – here we have a catalogue of qualities that would make the most gifted candidate for the episcopate quail. Mercifully, the report noted that this picture 'involves a diversity of gifts, not all of which can be looked for in a bishop, but which we must seek to ensure are present in their fulness in the episcopate as a body' (p. 288). However, the report does not actually say that a bishop should be a theologian.

What do the documents of the Second Vatican Council say about the theological ministry of a bishop? There are 119 entries in the index of the Abbott edition of the documents of Vatican II under 'Bishops', but no mention of theology in any of them.[6] There is, however, a good deal on the preaching and teaching ministry of bishops. They have Christ's authority to teach the faith and to ward off errors (p. 47; LG 25). This preaching and teaching ministry should have an apologetic slant; it should commend the faith in the light of modern circumstances and problems (p. 405; CD 13). Furthermore, it is the bishops' responsibility to ensure that there are theologians equipped to teach the faith to seminarians, clergy and laity (p. 572; PO 19).

The emphasis in Vatican II is on the teaching, sanctifying and governing roles of the bishop, the standard prophetic, priestly and pastoral aspects of episcopal ministry that we have already looked at. The bishop's responsibility, as defined in this Roman Catholic context, is to see that the authentic, inerrant teaching of the Church is handed on, that error is refuted, and that the Church is preserved in purity and truth. John Paul II, in his Apostolic Exhortation *Pastores Gregis*, following the Synod of Bishops in 2001, urged bishops to dialogue with theologians, but also reminded the bishops that they had the duty to

---

6. W. M. Abbott (ed.), *The Documents of Vatican II* (London and Dublin: Geoffrey Chapman, 1966); references in my main text.

evaluate the work of theologians in the light of Scripture and tradition.[7] Neither Vatican II nor John Paul II seem to explicitly recognize that to do theological work is part of the calling of every bishop. There is no sense there, or in the Church of England report on *Episcopal Ministry*, that the bishop is bound to wrestle with difficult questions, to explore mysteries and to launch out into the deeps of faith. So where is the prophetic dimension in the modern Roman Catholic understanding of episcopal ministry?

The Roman Catholic ecumenical theologian J. M. R. Tillard offered a stimulating discussion of the prophetic office of the bishop in his article 'How Is Christian Truth Taught in the Roman Catholic Church?'[8] Tillard goes beyond the institutional role that Vatican II sees for the bishop's teaching ministry. He is clear that the bishop's task is not that of mere 'faithful repetition'. It involves 'a constant re-reading' of the content of the Church's memory (living tradition) in order to facilitate its reception in the constantly evolving context of local churches (dioceses) and its transmission to the next generation, which needs to hear it in its own way. 'For, the Word of God being offered to the whole of humanity, it has to be heard and understood by all people of all time and cultures.' Tillard thus emphasizes the place of interpretation in teaching (p. 295).

When, however, Tillard comes to consider the role of theology more particularly, it turns out to be a rather tamed, controlled, somewhat instrumental understanding of theology that he proposes. Theology helps the Church to discover, confront and convincingly refute dangerous errors. It helps the Church to mediate the faith to diverse cultures. It serves spiritual contemplation of the truth of God. It enables discernment of new ideas to take place. And finally 'it guides it in the elaboration of its legislation by which rights are guarded and duties described with precision' (p. 200).

---

7. http://www.vatican.va/holy_father/john_paul_ii/apost_exhortations/ documents/hf_jp-ii_exh_20031016_pastores-gregis_en.html. Cf. Congregation for the Doctrine of the Faith (CDF), *Instruction*: Donum Veritatis, *On the Ecclesial Vocation of the Theologian* (1990), which stresses the quasi-infallibility of the Ordinary Magisterium, the duty of theologians to accept its teaching and the need to build trust between bishops and theologians: http://www.vatican.va/ roman_curia/congregations/cfaith/documents/rc_con_cfaith_doc_19900524 _theologian-vocation_en.html

8. J. M. R. Tillard, 'How Is Christian Truth Taught in the Roman Catholic Church?' *One in Christ*, XXXIV (1998), pp. 293–306 (page references in my main text).

William Telfer's study *The Office of a Bishop* has a chapter on 'Bishops and Theologians'.[9] Telfer argues that 'being a theologian is not among the necessary qualifications' of a person chosen to be a bishop. There is even, he suggests, some reason for thinking that theological gifts may not always be an asset. Though a bishop is called to form a judgement on theological issues and will need to provide himself with expert advisers, 'the task of theologians is different from that of the hierarchy. Theological thinking is exploratory thinking' (pp. 156 f). That nicely sharpens the issue that we are considering: can a bishop be also a theological explorer, or must a bishop be simply an exponent and defender of received tradition?

Acceptable exploring

The Durham affair spilt over into the Church of England's General Synod in 1985 and the House of Bishops produced a statement on the nature of Christian belief and the role of the bishop in relation to it.[10] The report took a conservative stance on the interpretation of the Creeds, but it was careful to allow scope for exploring different approaches:

> The questioning and creative process is a necessary part of Christian discipleship. Provided that it is positive, and undertaken out of concern for truth, with faith in the God who has brought us thus far, and with prayerful dependence on his Spirit, it will never be hurtful. In the past, crucial insights have been won by those who had the courage to question in faith. The Church of England is committed to this process with openness and integrity, and with a confidence, born of experience, that, however exacting it may be, essential truths of the Gospel will emerge from it more clearly understood. (p. 10: para. 12)

The report clearly did not exclude bishops from playing their part in these explorations, though it laid down certain safeguards:

> As teachers of the faith themselves, bishops need to be in sympathetic touch with those in the vanguard of knowledge. At the same time they need to distinguish in their own teaching between the well-established

9. William Telfer, *The Office of a Bishop* (London: Longmans, 1962).
10. House of Bishops of the General Synod of the Church of England, *The Nature of Christian Belief* (London: Church House Publishing, 1986).

fruits of scholarship and those more speculative and controversial hypotheses which have not yet been tested or found acceptance either in the scholarly community as a whole or within the Church. (p. 36: para. 70)

Furthermore:

Bishops... have to work under a discipline of mutual responsibility and accountability, and to be sensitive to traditional beliefs within the Church as well as to fresh insights. A bishop may properly enter into questionings on matters of belief... But in all he says he must take care not to present variant beliefs as if they were the faith of the Church. (p. 36: para. 70)

This is wise counsel, but some ambiguity remains. It seems that ambiguity is inescapable in the bishop's role as theologian. Every bishop is called to be a theologian (though not necessarily, of course, an academic one) because a bishop is ordained to teach the faith in a relevant way, to make judgements on the application of Scripture and tradition to topical issues and to enter into dialogue with those of different beliefs or none. The openness of the quest for truth and the negotiation that arises from dialogue are inevitably in tension with the bishop's office as the guardian of doctrine and teacher of the faith. How can this ambiguity be handled constructively? There can be no infallible recipe for this, but I offer a few points for reflection, which apply to all pastors and clergy but especially to bishops.

First, a foundation of trust needs to be built up between bishops and their people before they spring any theological surprises or advance any major challenges in the area of belief. Wise leaders build up their power base and give their people the opportunity to get to know them, to respect them and perhaps to hold them in affection.

Second, there is no need to confront people with all the issues at once. You can try to take them forward in their understanding a step at a time. Wise leaders avoid provocation. As they teach, they just turn the corner of the page, so to speak, in order that those who are ready may get a glimpse of what lies ahead. 'Those who have ears to hear, let them hear!'

Third, there is no call to issue outright challenges to aspects of belief that have already become moribund. Tilting at windmills is a sign of taking oneself too seriously. Let decaying beliefs wither on the vine. The Divine Right of Kings was once a central plank of Anglican faith. It passed away without the bishops (with one or two notorious exceptions) feeling called to attack it. Affirm what is good and true; let other items perish by neglect. Don't make those individuals who have never questioned their assumptions feel stupid and ignorant. When people become confused they feel threatened. When they are confronted by academic discourse they feel intimidated. Then you can count on some getting hold of the wrong end of the stick.

If I were a bishop called upon to give my views on a controversial theological question, I would try to follow the following rules. Make one point at a time. Use short sentences, avoiding subordinate clauses. Don't lapse into technical terms or in-group jargon. Look at the questioner and don't be evasive. Don't assume that you are under oath to give the whole picture, attempting to cover all facets of the subject. There is something to be said for what the Tractarians of the Oxford Movement called 'the doctrine of reserve in religious knowledge': spill the beans with care; 'cast not your pearls before swine'; take people forward step by step.

Finally, be positive. If you have to make a negative point, set it in a context of affirmation. Don't talk about 'What we can't believe', but about 'What we can believe'. Give reassuring signals to your audience by using familiar and traditional terms as far as possible. Explain your motives and so help to get people on your side. Always finish on a positive note. Build them up where their faith is sound. Even as you try to broaden their horizons, give people something to feed their faith. Then, I believe, they will be grateful to you and the bishop can indeed be a theologian.

Chapter 10

THE BISHOP IN THE PUBLIC SQUARE

The naked public square?

In 1984 the then Lutheran pastor (later a Roman Catholic priest) Richard John Neuhaus provoked intense debate when he published *The Naked Public Square: Religion and Democracy in America*.[1] Neuhaus challenged the prevailing secularist interpretation of the First Amendment to the American Constitution ('Congress shall make no law respecting an establishment of religion, or prohibiting the free exercise thereof; or abridging the freedom of speech, or of the press; or the right of the people peaceably to assemble, and to petition the government for a redress of grievances'). The original framers of the First Amendment (1791) were (he argued) seeking to guarantee religious liberty by not allowing one religion to be privileged over another. Churches were no longer to be established, as they were until then in several American states. Although the First Amendment was not intended to exclude religion from public life, successive applications of the Amendment, particularly rulings of the Supreme Court, were (Neuhaus argued) driving the progressive privatization of religion.[2] If faith did not belong

1. Richard John Neuhaus, *The Naked Public Square: Religion and Democracy in America* (Grand Rapids, MI: Eerdmans, 1984). On the overall theme of this chapter see Rowan Williams, *Faith in the Public Square* (London: Bloomsbury, 2012).

2. For substantiation of Neuhaus' point here see John Witte, 'The Study of Law and Religion in the United States: An Interim Report', *Ecclesiastical Law Journal*, 14 (2012), pp. 327–354, especially pp. 335–342. See also Richard J. Regan, *The American Constitution and Religion* (Washington, DC: The Catholic University of America Press, 2014). For a more British and global perspective see Roger Trigg, *Religion in Public Life: Must Faith Be Privatized?* (Oxford: Oxford University Press, 2007).

in the public domain, but was banished to the individual's personal life and the domestic sphere, he claimed, the public square would not remain empty – nature abhors a vacuum – and secular ideology would rush in to fill it. Neuhaus put his finger on the principle that, when Christians abdicate their public role, they simply make more space for non-Christian or anti-Christian doctrines to capture the limelight. Neuhaus rallied Christians to raise their voices in public debate in defence of Christian values and standards.

Wilfred M. McClay has put what Neuhaus was trying to do like this:

> to decouple liberal democracy from the iron logic of secularization ... to recover for public use an insight that was apparent to most of the Founders of the American republic – that the health of democratic institutions depends as much on the free and vibrant public presence of the biblical religions, and their culture-forming influence, as it does on the constraints placed on that religion's ability to exercise direct political power.[3]

McClay continues:

> A right understanding of Neuhaus' argument needs to balance both sides of this formulation. In other words, our choices should not be restricted – and in the end *cannot* be restricted – to either the complete privatization of religion or the complete integration of church and state. The separation of church and state is not, and cannot be, absolute, and it does not, and cannot, require the segregation of religion from public life ... it is a direct challenge to the idea that a commitment to official secularism as national policy is the logical, nay, inevitable, consequence of our commitment to liberal democracy.[4]

Anglican contexts

Although Neuhaus' initiative and all that flowed from it (including the journal *First Things*) were highly specific to the American context, they resonate more widely and have something to say to Anglican bishops in their various contexts, some of them, of course, far removed from the setting in which Neuhaus took up the struggle for Christian witness in

3. http://www.firstthings.com/article/2009/02/001-the-naked-public
4. http://www.firstthings.com/article/2009/02/001-the-naked-public

public affairs. The situations in which Anglican bishops exercise their ministry of leadership and witness vary enormously and include not only 'western' countries (even if they are in the Antipodes!), but Africa, the Middle East, South and East Asia and Latin America. Anglican bishops relate to various different regimes: under some, especially in Islamic countries, it is very difficult to make their voice heard at all; under others (notably the Church of England, which has bishops in the second chamber of the legislature, the House of Lords) they are given the opportunity to help to shape public policy.

For Anglican bishops in many countries, development issues and issues of social and economic justice will play a major part in their public role. Development will be an important vehicle for channelling what they say and do to apply Christian theological principles to their society. The Anglican Alliance and its staff are a resource that is available to offer support in this area.[5] A comprehensive, up-to-date, one-volume guide to the theory and practice of development is Bryant L. Myers, *Walking with the Poor: Principles and Practices of Transformational Development*.[6] In what follows now I will offer some theological principles or guidelines that I hope will prove relevant to the bishop's role in public affairs in most contexts throughout the Communion.

Church, state and society

If we trace through history the main lines of the Christian tradition on the relation of the Church to the state, we can discern several principles that can help to guide bishops in their role *vis-à-vis* the public square. These principles, that can be traced through biblical, medieval, Reformation, modern Roman Catholic and Anglican thought, are unfashionable today and receive little credence. The ideology of liberal relativism and multiculturalism is celebrated uncritically in western culture and now pervades public policy in many countries. This ideology has infiltrated the churches that have been directly shaped by the Reformation (so not the Roman Catholic and Orthodox churches) and has sapped their confidence in the tradition of Church–state interaction. The churches seem to be suffering from a loss of nerve to make bold and distinctive claims for the impact of the Christian revelation on national life, especially on moral issues and on social mores. But that may now be changing.

5. http://www.anglicancommunion.org/ministry/alliance/index.cfm
6. Revised and expanded edition, Maryknoll, NY: Orbis, 2011.

The Church's traditional language with regard to the relation between the Church and the state, which is broadly shared with some differences of emphasis by all the main Christian traditions, has been largely forgotten. It sounds strange even to Christian ears today. Twentieth-century totalitarian dictatorships, of the Right and of the Left (Nazism and Stalinism), perverted the idea of the state to evil ends, promoting demonic idolatry of the state and its leader. State, nation, leader and politics were fused into one. Constitutional checks and balances were abolished; critical distance was lost; costly prophetic critique was largely stifled. A combination of coercion and seduction brought some churches (notably the 'German Christians' and some Russian Orthodox) into this nexus. It is not surprising that, in liberal circles particularly, the language of the state and statehood has become rather suspect.

However, the idea of the state retains its validity, for all that. As Christian theology has long known, abuse does not destroy proper use. The existence of fanatical nationalism does not rule out true patriotism. Corrupt politics do not negate a political life that has integrity. Perverted ideology does not remove the need for a system of ideas and values that helps to bind people together. So it is with the theology of the state and the Church's relation to it. To retrieve this language from our Christian inheritance and to interpret its significance for today should not be merely an exercise in nostalgia. The central convictions that the tradition enshrines can be summarized concisely in the following points:[7]

1. The institution of the state in some form is ordained by God and is a creation ordinance. The well-being of humanity requires a stable political structure beyond the family and the local community, one that enables communities to relate to each other, to co-operate with each other, to protect the most vulnerable and to act together in a common purpose. The expression 'the state' stands for the enduring structure of governance, subsisting in various different historical forms and embodying ideals of the common good – that is to say, of vocation, mutual responsibility, vicarious service and accountability.

7. These concise points are expanded with supporting evidence from the Bible and the Christian theological tradition in Paul Avis, *Church, State and Establishment* (London: SPCK, 2001). See also Mark Chapman, Judith Maltby and William Whyte (eds), *Established Church: Past, Present and Future* (London and New York: T&T Clark, 2011); David Fergusson, *Church, State and Civil Society* (Cambridge: Cambridge University Press, 2004).

2. The theological truth that the proper role of the state belongs to the will of God for human well-being needs to be re-affirmed today in view of the prevalent scepticism in the West about the very idea of the state and the endemic distrust and apathy with regard to national, regional and local government, combined with the comparative weakness of the institutions that make up civil society. (The expression 'civil society' refers to all the institutions that are located between the family on the one hand and the state on the other: institutions to do with education, health care, voluntary welfare organizations, heritage, environment, the arts and many more.) At a time when all inherited institutions tend to be viewed with suspicion, Christians may need reminding that, like the Church of Christ itself, the state is in principle a God-given institution.

3. The state as an institution needs to be distinguished from any particular government that happens to be in power and from the sway of political parties. Particular, transitory political regimes are not ordained by God but are permitted in God's providence. Just as the structures of the Church can fail and become corrupt, so that it needs reform and renewal, so too the powers of the state can be perverted by evil or misguided regimes. Nevertheless, the state should be honoured, served and defended. We should actively interest ourselves in the constitutional, legal foundation of the state within which, we live. Bishops should encourage and promote civic and political responsibility and engagement on the part of their people.

4. Those who serve the state, like those who serve the Church, are doing God's good work. Like the sacred ministry of the Church, the service of the state remains God's work even when carried out in an inadequate or unworthy manner or for the wrong motives. There is a Christian calling to serve the community in a representative way through the structures of governance that comprise the state. Earlier Christian writers sometimes put the ordained ministry of word and sacrament and the ministry of governance in the state on a par: both were God-given vocations. The fact that the comparison seems far-fetched, if not ludicrous today is a measure of how far Church and society have drifted from their moorings in the Christian tradition. Politicians in general have a deplorable public image, though the public perception of the clergy (in Europe particularly) affords no grounds for complacency. Public trust in both politicians and

clergy is distressingly low in some societies. However, the principle that those who offer themselves in the service of the state, to work for the common good, are serving God's good purposes and actually doing 'God's work' remains true. I do not think I have ever heard that truth explicitly stated by Church leaders at the time of a General Election in the UK. Yet that principle helps to explain why we believe we should expect a high standard of personal conduct and of professional accountability in our elected politicians who are called to serve the commonwealth.

5. Every human society needs a foundation in transcendent truths and values. A merely functional or instrumental justification for the state is inadequate. The state does not exist simply to 'hold the ring' between competing power groups and ideologies, including religions, or to provide merely for the material or even the cultural needs of its people. The state should be seen as a coherent entity, as a sort of corporate moral person. It has moral responsibilities and is morally accountable in the persons of its elected representatives. Politicians are among its servants. They therefore have an obligation to serve the ends and uphold the values that are intrinsic to the state, not merely to promote their own personal advantage and career goals. The prevailing liberal relativism that holds that people should be free to live as they please provided that they do not thereby inflict harm on others is not robust enough to sustain a coherent society, especially in times of tension and conflict such as those that we live in today in the early twenty-first century.

6. In order to flourish, and even to survive, a society needs to commit itself publicly to certain goals – goals that are inevitably long-term ones – and to acknowledge values that transcend individual fulfilment and selfish gratification. These aims and values include compassionate care for the less fortunate; a sense of moral obligation to others and to the community; privileging the primary, irreplaceable relationships of marriage and parenthood and supporting stable relationships, especially in family life; making a safe space for minorities, whether of belief or of lifestyle; recognizing the value of self-discipline and restraint; and encouraging the ideals of belonging and serving that build up a community. These goals and values are all grounded in Scripture and upheld by traditional Christian teaching. The Church should be the first to challenge the corrosive cultural paradigm of 'the privatization of values', but in practice it often colludes with it, retreating to the cultural margins.

7. If the state is intrinsically underpinned by transcendent, spiritual and moral truths, the concept of a secular state is really a contradiction in terms. A state cannot be without ultimate values, concerns and commitments. It cannot be neutral with regard to what matters most. Moral truths and values are sustained by moral communities. A nation is a major moral community. The common good needs to be realized at the level of the state as well as in local communities, civil society and in the international order. When earlier Christian theologians assumed that every state upholds a certain religion, even if not the Christian one, that was not merely a sociological observation. Beliefs that evoke the transcendent and values that look beyond the demands of individual consumption and the constraints of the current electoral term are essential for a healthy society. The Christian Church, for all its failings, offers precisely these beliefs and values on the basis of divine revelation and can therefore speak with conviction and without apology. There are millions of people in our societies today who long for the Church to speak these truths clearly and boldly. Though such a move would generate opposition from some, it would evoke respect and gratitude from many others.

8. As twin divinely ordained institutions – two channels through which God is at work for the well-being of God's human creatures – the Church and the state must relate to each other. They cannot ignore each other's existence. They have mutual obligations and should, therefore, seek to reach an arrangement that respects the calling and integrity of each. The Church should not attempt to usurp the role of the state by claiming jurisdiction over the temporal aspects of society as it did in the Middle Ages (and more recently in the case of the Roman Catholic Church). The state should not attempt to dominate or control the Church or to usurp its spiritual authority. The Church should have the freedom (under the law of the land, which applies to all citizens) to take responsibility for its doctrine, worship, discipline and appointments. But that cannot mean that there is no interaction between the Church and the state. Some kind of mutual responsibility and mutual engagement on the part of the Church and the state is almost universally accepted by the churches, whether they enjoy some form of establishment or not.

9. By virtue of its obligation to ensure the moral and spiritual well-being of its people, the state may give formal recognition, in law and in the constitution (written or unwritten), to the Christian

religion in the form of one or more churches. In many countries churches are now required to register with the state: this in itself is a form of mutual recognition. This recognition provides the Church – to varying degrees, depending on the context – with various opportunities for pastoral, prophetic and priestly engagement with the community. The Church cannot renounce this engagement without betraying its mission. Such recognition helps it to bring its ministry to bear on the life of the nation at every level: in local communities; in the numerous institutions that make up civil society; and nationally, in debates on public policy. The Church's contribution will not always be heeded, but it is true that to speak and sometimes be ignored is better than to be structurally marginalized and socially invisible.

10. The state dimension of the Church's mission is related to its other dimensions. The pastoral ministry, in all the local communities and the many sector ministries (chaplaincies) that relate to institutions, underpins and validates the message that the Church seeks to put across at the national level. The local, the institutional (civil society) and the national dimensions of the Church's mission interlock. An effective mission in the sphere of civil society will be hampered in the absence of active engagement with the state. For the Church of England, uniquely in the Anglican Communion, though not uniquely in Christendom, the territorial scope (though not, of course, the apostolic mandate) of the ministry of the priest in the parish and of the bishop in the diocese, to all in the community who are willing to receive it, depends on the church's establishment in law (Canon C 18).

11. This combination of mutual recognition and mutual obligation on the part of Church and state – colloquially referred to as 'establishment' – takes many forms and undergoes continual modification and negotiation. The Concordats and similar agreements that the Roman Catholic Church has with many states (well over 100) are a particular form of establishment in that sense. Establishment is not in principle incompatible with a plural society where the role of other faith communities is also acknowledged in law and in practice. For example, the Church of England can value the fact that it is 'by law established' while at the same time working closely with other churches and faiths and advocating that they should have a greater voice in public discourse (e.g. in the House of Lords). The Church of England does not seek a religious monopoly and in any case its monopoly was broken two centuries

ago. It is partly because the Church of England is established
that it is a tolerant, comprehensive church. The Roman Catholic
Church can welcome Concordats while upholding, as Vatican II
did, the principle of religious freedom. Lutheran churches in the
Nordic lands can retain a special relationship with the state while
seeking to respond to new reality of religious pluralism. The tension
between state recognition and pluralism is not simply an issue of
late modernity, but has been around for centuries. A sophisticated
constitutional model, combining tolerance of diverse faith
communities with special, historic affirmation of one in particular
for the benefit of all, is possible, provided that that one itself
supports and practises the values of tolerance, openness to dialogue
and hospitality.

12. What is true for many Anglican Churches is that the radical
privatization of values and the uncritical praise of pluralism and
multiculturalism, that has eclipsed the traditional view of Church
and society in western culture, appears extremely threadbare in
the light of 11 September 2001 and the ongoing terrorist threat.
People cannot combine to work together for the common good and
against a common threat on the basis of sheer individual preference
that brooks no interference. What is needed to sustain a coherent
society is a set of communal values that are publicly owned and are
instantiated in local communities, in the institutions and voluntary
organizations of civil society and, at the national level, in the
legal framework of the state. The building of community – moral
community – becomes a priority. As major moral communities
within the nations, the churches are probably the most effective
sustainers of those transcendent values that have objectivity over
against selfish individual preference – and the bishops are in the
vanguard of this mission.

13. The Church's constructive relation to the state is an aspect of the
mission that it has received from God. The Church is called to serve
the *missio dei*, God's purpose of righteousness and love that unfolds
in history and is centred on Jesus Christ and his Kingdom. The
Church announces the sovereign claim of God over every aspect of
life and seeks to bring all forms of human existence under the reign
of God. This mission requires engagement, preferably partnership,
with the state, provided that the essential integrity of the Church,
as the Body of Christ under his headship, is not compromised.
A relationship of engaged partnership between the Church and the
state is not the same as identifying one with the other or blurring

the boundary between them. A critical tension is maintained. Such a vigilant partnership is neither Erastianism (state domination of the Church) nor theocracy (rule by clerics). Given that vital safeguard, the principle of Church–state co-operation (and the various forms that it takes in different countries and among all the historic Christian traditions) should be thankfully affirmed, without any hint of apology or defensiveness.

On the basis of these broad theological principles, which apply, I think, in most, if not all, contexts, Anglican bishops can take up their role in public affairs with confidence and integrity as various opportunities come their way. They can do that in the consciousness that by so doing they are fulfilling their ordination mandate as a bishop in mission, spearheading the mission of the people of God and working for the well-being of all God's children, outside as well as inside the Church.

Chapter 11

THE BISHOP AND THE LITURGY

The liturgy – The bishop's proper work

It is in the liturgy that the bishop is most truly the bishop.[1] The bishop's place is at the heart of the Church's worship. When the bishop presides at the celebration of the Eucharist in the midst of his or her people, the nature of episcopal ministry is seen most clearly. And this is particularly true if the worship is taking place in the cathedral, the seat of the bishop. In the Eucharist the people of God, as the body of Christ, are drawn into the movement of the Lord's self-offering to the Father – that great act of total self-oblation from the beginning to the end of his earthly ministry, that culminated in the sacrifice of the cross and continues eternally in heaven. Sharing in Christ's threefold messianic anointing as Prophet, Priest and King, the Church's primary tasks (as we have noted) are to teach, to sanctify and to govern. These three tasks come into focus in ordered, Spirit-filled worship. In serving the liturgy of the Church the bishop is fulfilling his or her special ministry in relation to the triple task of the Church: teaching the word of God, celebrating the sacraments and exercising pastoral oversight, for all three functions are operative in episcopal presidency at the Eucharist. When bishops take their proper place in liturgical presidency, at the altar of God, they know that they have come home: 'This is where I belong.' Where the people of God are gathered for worship there is a bishop-shaped liturgical space waiting to be filled. So let the bishops

---

1. Relevant resources on the topic of this chapter include: Colin Buchanan (ed.), *The Bishop in Liturgy* (Bramcote: Grove Books, 1988) especially the essays by John Halliburton, David Stancliffe and Michael Perham; Susan K. Wood, 'A Liturgical Theology of the Episcopacy', in David A. Stosur (ed.), *Unfailing Patience and Sound Teaching: Reflections on Episcopal Ministry in Honor of Rembert G. Weakland, O.S.B.* (Collegeville, MI: Liturgical Press, 1993), pp. 31–44.

occupy it with joy. As Paul writes to a young quasi-bishop, 'Make full proof of thy ministry' (2 Timothy 4.5, KJB).

The liturgy is literally the Church's work (*leiturgia*) – what it does for God and for the world. To worship the Father, through the Son, in the power of the Spirit and in the face of the world is what the Church is here for. The gathered Christian community celebrates the sacraments under the leadership, guidance and authority of the one who presides. If the liturgy is the Church's proper work, it is also the bishop's proper work. When the bishop is present, whether in a parish church of the diocese or in the cathedral, the bishop presides (unless the metropolitan, the archbishop, is present). But that does not mean that the bishop (or any other president) should do everything in person: the president is not a factotum. Much can be delegated (though not certain items – the opening greeting, the collect, the absolution, the peace, the Eucharistic prayer and the blessing – which are all presidential acts).[2] Presiding at worship is the principal way that the bishop can model good liturgical practice for the clergy and people of the diocese. In particular, at the Chrism Eucharist on Maundy Thursday, at which the Holy Oils are blessed, the bishop gathers the ministers of the diocese – fellow bishops, priests and deacons (and in some Anglican Churches Readers and other licensed lay ministers). Here a sense of collegiality and mutual support can be evoked.

Mutual care and support

Without their bishop and his or her clergy, Christian people are like sheep without a shepherd. By the same token, without his or her clergy and people, a bishop is a beached whale, an inflated ecclesiastic without a role. People and pastor need each other in order to be themselves; they must come together to form the Church. In the Anglican understanding of the Church, pastors are integral to the Church; the apostolic ministry is ecclesiologically constitutive; it goes to make the Church what it is. The Reformation taught that word and sacrament identify where the true church is to be found (cf. Article XIX of the Thirty-Nine Articles). But word and sacrament do not minister themselves: they cannot happen without human agency and they need human oversight. Pastors

2. Cf. David R. Holeton (ed.), *Renewing the Anglican Eucharist: Findings of the Fifth International Anglican Liturgical Consultation, Dublin, Eire, 1995* (Cambridge: Grove Books, 1996), pp. 20–21.

and people need each other and should offer and receive mutual care. The bishop may sometimes feel like the flying buttress that is semi-detached but props up the church or cathedral. Actually without the church the buttress would collapse. The bishop needs his/her people. It is an important moment of insight, of breakthrough, when we realize for the first time, 'I need them more than they need me.'

It is ecclesiologically appropriate that the diocesan bishop should be named in the liturgical intercessions (before the metropolitan, heads of other Christian churches, or the local clergy and certainly before the head of state), if no explicit provision is made for the bishop to be mentioned in the Eucharistic prayer. However, in my experience, parishes are generally poor at remembering to pray for their bishop by name, and members of the congregation who lead the intercessions often seem inadequately prepared or briefed. It does not seem to occur to many people that their bishop has anything much to do with what goes on in the parish church Sunday by Sunday. They do not realize that without the bishop there would be no functioning church there, no clergy and no sacraments. But above all, the bishop actually needs the prayers of the people. How can she/he go on in ministry unless sustained by the ongoing prayers of the faithful? Every bishop should feel this in their heart; the bishop who does not have this sense is on dangerous ground spiritually. So it does not come at all amiss, when the bishop is ministering in a particular parish, for them to remind the people that they need a secure place in their common prayer. Among Pope Francis' first public words were, 'Pray for me.'

Catholicity

Sacramental worship is not merely the act of a particular local gathering. The liturgy is always the act of the whole Church. This is particularly clear when the bishop presides – it brings out the catholicity of the act. So Rowan Williams suggests that the bishop's role and function 'is essentially to enable the community to state in ritual form its unity in the crucified and risen Christ (and thus also its freedom from exclusively local prejudice and interest – its catholicity).'[3] The catholicity of the

---

3. Rowan Williams, 'Authority and the Bishop in the Church', in Mark Santer (ed.), *Their Lord and Ours: Approaches to Authority, Community and the Unity of the Church*; Foreword by the Archbishop of Canterbury [Robert Runcie] (London: SPCK, 1982) p. 98.

liturgical event is also manifested when the bishop ordains deacons and priests (preferably not in the same service) in his or her cathedral: the universality of their orders is underlined. But it is also true of the sacraments of baptism and Eucharist. Baptism is not initiation into a particular denomination, but into the universal Church, the one body (1 Corinthians 12.13): that is the catholicity of baptism. Similarly, a Eucharistic liturgy is one particular celebration of the catholic Eucharist. There is only one Eucharist, in which Jesus Christ is the priest who offers, the offering that is made and the food that is received, but the one Eucharist is manifested in a multitude of individual celebrations every day from the rising of the sun to its setting (Malachi 1.11).

Least of all should the liturgy be seen as a sort of virtuoso performance by the person presiding – 'Look at me! See how I do it.' God forbid. The president – whether bishop or priest (and the bishop is exercising a priestly, as well as an episcopal ministry here) – is simply the *diakonos*, the minister, agent or servant of God, of God's Church and of God's world in facilitating the liturgy. In the spirit of St Francis of Assisi we sing, 'Make me a channel of your peace.' The president longs to be invisible, to be obliterated, in order to make room for the Lord of the Church. Like the figure of John the Baptist in the early sixteenth-century Isenheim altarpiece (by the mysterious artist known as 'Grünewald'), with his elongated index finger, the bishop points away from self to Christ crucified under the rubric, 'He must increase, but I must decrease' (John 3.30).

The liturgy preaches the gospel

Above all, the liturgy shows forth the good news of Jesus Christ. It tells of his incarnation, ministry, suffering, death, resurrection, ascension and the sending of the Holy Spirit – together with the promise and hope of the fulfilment of God's loving and just purposes for the creation in the last days. The words and actions of the liturgy are filled with the gospel. Both the baptism and the Eucharist narrate the gospel and do so in dramatic mode. Baptism speaks of Christ's descent into the waters of the Jordan and of his rising up to receive the power of the Spirit. It tells also of his immersion in the deep waters of death and his rising again in the power of an indestructible life (Hebrews 7.16). And these two events, his immersion–anointing and his crucifixion–resurrection, at the beginning and at the end of his public ministry, are one reality. Baptism enables us to share, by faith and sacrament, in this mystery.

'Therefore we have been buried with him by baptism into death, so that, just as Christ was raised from the dead by the glory of the Father, so we too might walk in newness of life' (Romans 6.4). The Eucharist also tells of the mighty acts of God in salvation history, culminating in the coming of Jesus Christ, and especially – in the bread and wine – it speaks of his death and resurrection. 'For as often as you eat this bread and drink the cup, you proclaim the Lord's death until he comes' (1 Corinthians 11.26). As Michael Ramsey tersely puts it in *The Gospel and the Catholic Church*, 'The liturgy declares the Gospel of God.'[4] It not only declares it, but it also enables us to participate in it and to receive its benefits. In presiding at the liturgy the bishop becomes once more an evangelist, a herald of the gospel of Christ.

The bishop is not a visitor

The bishop's visitation of a parish, perhaps for a confirmation service, will be a high point for the congregation. Weeks of planning and preparation will have gone into the smooth running of the service, the arrangements for hospitality, etc. The congregation will be larger than usual, children will probably be more visible and everyone will be on their best behaviour. Backbiting will be subdued, the choir will have had adequate practice and people will arrive at church in good time. All will be sweetness and light. The bishop knows that this display is the exception that proves the rule. She/he needs someone – like the medieval court jester whose job it was to bring kings down to earth – to whisper that it is not like this every week! The hard struggle will resume in the parish once the bishop's car has disappeared round the corner of the street.

The clergy, the churchwardens, the chair of the vestry, etc. will want to warmly 'welcome' the bishop to the parish, but this would be an ecclesiological *faux pas*. The bishop is not 'visiting' the parish and is not a guest to be 'welcomed'. The bishop belongs to the parish and the parish belongs to the bishop. The clergy are the bishop's representatives and colleagues. As the bishop says to the new parish priest in some Anglican Churches: 'Receive the cure of souls which is both mine and yours.' Bishops are, by the nature of their office, the 'principal ministers' of word and sacrament within the portion of the people of

4. A. M. Ramsey, *The Gospel and the Catholic Church* (London: Longmans, Green & Co., 1936), p. 108.

God committed to their care, and have the oversight of the ministry of word, sacrament and pastoral care throughout the diocese. Bishop and parish are integral to each other. So, in more ways than one, the bishop in a parish has 'come home'.

It is proper practice for the bishop to preside at the Eucharist when in a parish of the diocese or in the cathedral. It is not merely hierarchy or deference that dictates that the bishop should always preside at the Eucharist and that the bishop should give the absolution and the blessing at a non-Eucharistic service, and that the bishop should bring up the rear in a liturgical procession. It is ecclesiology – the bishop's role in the Church – that determines this and in particular the concept of oversight. In the same way, it is by virtue of the same theological principle, the principle of oversight (*episkope*), that the bishop should decide (well in advance) what will happen in the service: the format, content, choice of rite and music and who will do what, though with sensitivity to local custom. The bishop must approve how the service is put together.

An evangelistic opportunity

Many Christians who do not come to church very regularly will crawl out of the woodwork to see the bishop and to be seen by him or her. If the service is a confirmation or an ordination, family members and friends of the candidates will be present in numbers. They may be unfamiliar both with the order of service and with its meaning. Many will not have much of a clue about what confirmation or ordination is. They may not even have more than a very hazy idea of what the Church is all about. Much may be completely new and strange to them. Here is an enormous missionary opportunity for the bishop, one to seize with both hands: aiming to leave them attracted by what they have experienced, wanting to know more and clear about the steps that they should take. The liturgy of Christian initiation, at a Confirmation service, is a golden opportunity. The stages of initiation into the life of grace in the Church are laid out: catechesis (first in the case of adults and later in the case of infants), baptism, confirmation and first communion (or communion before confirmation, but after preparation). Those who are drawn to enquire, either then or later, will see what God in God's goodness has already done for the candidates and can do also for them. What the grace of God has in store for them is a step by wonderful step induction into the holy mysteries in which, by the mercy of God, the bishop is called to preside.[5]

Vesture and protocols

It would not be appropriate to go into any detail about what the bishop should wear and other protocols of episcopal ministry in parish church and cathedral. Vesture and protocols will vary according to the tradition of the particular Anglican Church, the inclinations of the bishop and local custom. Some Churches provide guidelines for their bishops. The guidelines that the Church of England offers are available at www. transformingworship.org.uk, but of course these would not be suitable everywhere or for all.

The bishop and the healing ministry

As part of their leadership role in mission, it is fitting for bishops to take a lead in the Church's healing ministry. This ministry takes place through prayer, anointing with holy oil and the laying on of hands. Bishops carry out this ministry 'after the manner of the holy Apostles' (as the Book of Common Prayer, 1662, Confirmation service puts it), because the twelve and St Paul were engaged in healing the sick and so left an example to those, the bishops, who inherit the apostolic ministry. In the New Testament, the same word (sozo) means 'I save' and 'I heal': healing and salvation are two ways of expressing the same reality of grace. Jesus sent his disciples to preach the gospel and heal the sick (Luke 9.2; 10.9). This twofold mandate reflects the truly embodied nature of human wholeness. The gospel brings the healing of human identity in its totality – body, mind and spirit.[6]

At a service of wholeness and healing it is good practice for the bishop to share the laying on of hands with a fellow priest or with a lay person with a healing gift, whose ministry in this area is recognized

5. See further, Paul Avis (ed.), *The Journey of Christian Initiation: Theological and Pastoral Perspectives* (London: Church House Publishing, 2011).

6. For further exposition of this theme see Paul Avis, *A Church Drawing Near: Spirituality and Mission in a Post-Christian Context* (London and New York: T&T Clark, 2003), chapter 2. I am grateful to the Revd Elizabeth Baxter and Gill White for advice in this area.

and accepted in the community. While it belongs particularly to the ministry of priests (and therefore bishops), who are ordained to the sacramental ministry of reconciliation, to minister Christ's healing power, we need to recognize that any Christian can receive from God a special gift of healing, often exercised through 'healing hands'. It would be seriously remiss of the Church not to recognize and use such gifts. The important principle is that the ministry be shared, to avoid giving the impression that it all depends on one person and that that person is the bishop.

It sets an example of proper humility (as well as of humanity) if the one presiding at a healing service (in this case the bishop) first receives the laying on of hands with a prayer for healing and wholeness from the priest, deacon or lay person who is working with him or her; and then the reverse. This action speaks volumes about the equal need of all the participating ministers for Christ's healing touch. 'My need is as great as yours.' It makes a very clear statement that healing power comes from elsewhere, 'from above', not from the minister as a human individual. Unless the person presiding at the healing service (the bishop in this case) constantly feels their own need of God-given wholeness, they are in the wrong role. They must be fully content to be a 'wounded healer'.

It is not generally necessary for the minister (bishop) to know what ails the person seeking healing. It is enough that God knows their condition. There is no need for a whispered medical consultation at the altar rail. Give no space to prying or prurience. Knowledge is power; increasing the imbalance of power between the minister and the one being ministered to is not what is wanted in this situation. It can also be made clear that people can come to receive prayer for healing on behalf of another who is not present at the service – by proxy, so to speak. Their names (Christian names only) can be mentioned in the intercessions that precede the laying on of hands. Contrary to the view of some, I cannot see why anointing, as well as prayer and the laying on of hands, cannot be received by proxy – it is not as though anointing imparts a sacramental 'character', as baptism, confirmation, ordination and marriage do in catholic sacramental theology.[7]

It is the Lord's power that we want to convey, not our own ego. We will not want to get in the Lord's way, but instead simply to 'prepare the way of the Lord', as John the Baptist did. Therefore we will be gentle with our

---

7. Contra Andrew Davison, *Why Sacraments?* (London: SPCK, 2013), p. 124; but his discussion of anointing is generally helpful.

touch, perhaps resting the hand on the shoulder, rather than on the head. After a pause, the minister (bishop) can raise the person by taking their hand, if it is offered. There should be no hint of mediating patriarchal power when male bishops minister to women in need of physical, mental or spiritual strength. It is enough to be a channel of God's peace. A suitable prayer at this point of the healing service might be:

> In the name of our Lord Jesus Christ, who laid his hands on the sick that they might be healed, I lay my hands upon you now. May almighty God, Father, Son and Holy Spirit, make you and those in your prayers whole, give you light and peace, and keep you in eternal life. Amen.

INDEX OF NAMES